SEXUAL
IN
OTTOMAN SOCIETY

SEXUAL LIFE
IN
OTTOMAN SOCIETY

Sema Nilgün Erdoğan

DÖNENCE
İSTANBUL

SEXUAL LIFE IN OTTOMAN SOCIETY
Sema Nilgün Erdoğan

Written by	: Sema Nilgün Erdoğan
Cover	: Fatih M. Durmuş
Photos by	: Dönence Diabank Archives
Printed in Turkey by	Müka Matbaacılık – İstanbul

IOSB, Sinpaş İş Modern E10 Başakşehir / İstanbul - Türkiye
T: +90 212 549 68 24   Certificate No: 12219

ISBN 975-7054-00-3
7th edition 2013

Published and distributed by

Dönence Basım ve Yayın Hizmetleri
Çatalçeşme Sokak, 15/2 Cağaloğlu
İstanbul/ TÜRKİYE
Tel.: (90 212) 511 18 89
Fax: (90 212) 511 58 83
E-mail: donenceyay@hotmail.com

CONTENTS

SEXUAL LIFE IN OTTOMAN SOCIETY

The Ottoman Empire was a Muslim state and the strict rules of this religion were reflected on sexual life.

The family was inviolable and virginity was untouchable. Human reproduction was a sacred duty. Therefore, males were just creatures who accomplished nature's act of procreation and women were regarded to be human beings who could not help being driven by their strong sexual needs. Although this biological urge was restricted by religion, tolerance could still penetrate into these precise circumscriptions. Sexual deviations which are observed in human beings were taken into consideration as well.

The holy book Koran implies that the sexual act is necessary for the continuity of the race, but during intercourse only the male has the right to express his sexual excitement and get full satisfaction. The female is under some restrictions; in that she has to be moderate and reasonable. The wife and husband were obliged to do whatever has to be done in bed; because this was an unavoidable moral duty and was essential for the continuity of marriage.

The Ottoman male could have four women as his legal wives by permission of the Koran. This question has always been on the agendas of contemporary men interested in this subject. Why can not they have more than one wife like the privileged Ottomans, is there anything wrong with them?

In earlier times, this was a precaution taken to prevent prostitution. It also kept men at home which led to the increase of the Muslim population.

Islamic rules favor men as a result, and Islamic countries are mostly male-dominated societies.

The Koran also says that either partner can ask for a divorce. However, it was easier for an Ottoman man to find reasons to get rid of the woman he no longer fancied. A woman could only ask for divorce under the condition that her husband asked her to perform perverted sexual intercourse or, when he no longer could provide satisfaction with his male organ.

In the Ottoman society, family life was rather secluded and this is evident in civil architecture. The section where women lived was called 'Harem' and it was the prohibited area. No one other than the family members could enter this place.

Because of strict rules and restrictions, the development of a healthy relationship between men and women was inhibited and some sexual deviations were inevitable. We have very few written texts on Ottoman Sexual Life which have survived. The existing texts deal with male and female homosexuality beside intersexual relationships though in a colorful manner.

In spite of all the contradictions in the written documents or in social behavior related to sex, there existed some tolerance that softened the harsh rules of practiced Islam surprisingly.

Perhaps this tolerance came from the Palace, from the Sultans themselves filled with all the pleasures of carnality, who might have had their eyes half-closed. ,

Some sections of this book are extractions from written documents which were published very recently. I would like to express my gratitude to editors Çağatay Uluçay, Murat Bardakçı and Ergun Hiçyılmaz who gave us the opportunity to form a mental picture of the Ottoman way of life by bringing those erotic books under light after a lot of hard work.

Now you are alone with the erotic reading matter. Let it be your companion full of excitement and amusement.

May tolerance be by your side.
The Editor

THE GREATEST MYSTERY: HAREM

Harem, one of the most enigmatic words of the Ottoman culture from the far east to the deepest west has always been a subject of interest for both men and women.

Literally, Harem means 'the women's quarters of a Muslim household. In obedience to Muslim religion which prohibits women from being seen by non-related men, Ottoman men of sufficient means including the Sultans had to build separate quarters in their residences for their wives, children and slaves.

Women spent their lives in private locations with their children and female slaves. In Ottoman residences, there were also special rooms for men to host their guests which are called 'Birun' or 'Selamlık'. The only connection between Haremlik and Selamlık was a door and there were corridors and very thick walls between them.

Nevertheless, today when the name 'Harem' is mentioned what comes to mind is the Harem of the Ottoman Sultans in the Topkapı Palace, which was also called The House of Joy (Dar'üs Saade), and this heaven which was filled up with the most outstanding beauties of all colors from all over the world was possessed by one man only, the Sultan. Can you imagine a more glorious dream than this treasure?

The number of women in the Sultan's Harem was never less than 300, and this number increased to 900 in the 19lh century. In the Harem of the Topkapı Palace, almost 1000 people lived including the slaves and other servants.

The mystery of the Harem has always been an up to date topic for some Western writers. They tried to picture this fabulous establishment mainly with the help of their imagination.

What you will read here is all based on actual documents, and the events and people are described by eyewitnesses.

We shall now have a glimpse of this forbidden city (or this artificial heaven) which actually had very strict rules. Its inhabitants sometimes had a vital effect on Ottoman politics.

Everything started in the year 1365 when Sultan Murad I deci-

Cariyes by the swimming pool of the Palace. Jéan Leon Gérôme, 1886

ded to have a palace fit to reflect his sovereignty, so a palace was built in Edirne (Adrianople) which was the capital of the Ottoman Empire at that time. The Palace was called 'Cihannuma Kasri'. However the true meaning of the palace institution and Harem emerged after Fatih Sultan Mehmet conquered Istanbul in 1453.

The most famous imperial palace in Istanbul is the Topkapı Palace but there are many other palaces and pavilions used for different purposes at different times of the year.

Ottoman Palaces were surrounded with huge gardens which were very well taken care of. They were adorned with pools and fine ornaments. In this paradise were gathered the red-haired, white-skinned beauties from Ireland to almond-eyed Indian beauties playing the part of the angels.

10

The Sultans and their viziers were very pleased when a distinguished beauty was presented to them as a gift. So some people who meant to pay a very special homage to the Sultans sometimes traveled all over the world and bought off pretty girls from their families to present them to the Palace.

Slave traders had an important function in enlarging this unique collection too.

The Sultan rested in the kiosk decorated with ivy in the meadows, shadowed by the aged trees and watched the nymphs in laces embraced by the sweet scent of jasmine until dawn.

THE MAIN CHARACTERS IN THE HAREM SCENE

Valide Sultan: (Mother of the Sultan) She was the ruler of the Harem and came after the Sultan. Since the Sultans sometimes ascended the throne at a very young age, she became the ruler of the Empire as well.

Baş Kadın Efendi: (Baş Haseki) Mother of the Sultan's first child and the "apple" of the Sultan's eye.

İkballer: These were the women who gave birth to the Sultan's children after the first child. They were considered to be the wives. Their number was at least four an 4 at most seven.

Gedikli Kadınlar: These were the experienced slaves who gave the most intimate service to the Sultan. Giving the Sultan his bath was one of their duties.

Odalıklar: (Odalisks) The young slaves with whom the Sultan spent his nights were the future mothers of his children.

Gözde: The beautiful young slave girls, who managed to attract the Sultan's attraction and shared his bed.

Cariyeler: They were the maids of the Harem. If they were fortunate enough and had the qualifications, they advanced to the level of 'Gözde'.

Black Eunuchs: They were the kidnapped children of Abyssinia and Sudan, who were castrated by special methods to be the guardians of the Harem. They were responsible for communication with the outside world. Kızlarağası ("The Chief Captain of the girls") was the chief of the black eunuchs. He also arranged the promotions of women and selected the new slave girls, which was a very important duty because the slave girls had to have a perfectly built figure in order to be a member of the Harem. After being selected by the Kızlarağası, young slave girls were also examined by the Başkadın Efendi and were disciplined and trained by experienced slaves. The training included music, literature and all kinds of social graces. They had to complete this education successfully because it was the only passage to the Sultan's bed.

A new member of the Harem had only one aim, and that was to be desired by the Sultan; so in order to achieve her goal she dressed up, adorned herself, and if she had a chance to catch the attraction of the Sultan she used every means to display her charms. Thus, she could have the chance to be the wife of the most powerful Emperor of the world. What a dream and destiny must that be for a village girl whose only merit was her physical beauty.

If I were in her shoes and if the only merit I had was my beauty, I would do anything to change my destiny, at whatever cost there may be.

The Sultan never exhibited his admiration for a new slave girl but his servant who would be walking behind him sensed his interest from the look in the Sultan's eye and immediately sent a message to the Kızlarağası, so that he could prepare the new girl for the Sultan's bed. Then, the lucky girl was taken to the Turkish bath (hamam) with the other slave girls. All the extra body hair was waxed and she was washed, fragranced and adorned and taken to the Sultan's bedroom as they sang songs and played their instruments.

The girl entered the room alone and crept toward the Sultan's bed and got into the bed from the side where his feet were located. Her first night with the Sultan could also be the first day of her glory because she could either get pregnant and give him a son and become a legal wife, or she could put her spell on the Sultan with her charm and excellence in love-making and become one of his constant favorites.

FESTIVITIES IN THE GARDENS OF THE PALACE

Sultan Selim II, who ruled the Ottoman Empire between the years 1566 and 1574, enjoyed hunting and so he resided in the

12

Birth in the Harem, Miniature from Zenannâme, 18th century, İ.Ü. Library.

Palace in Edirne (Adrianople) on the banks of the Tunca River, during his hunting sessions. When the Sultan wished to be joyous, he gave orders to his servants and they carried the drinks and food into the garden. After sunset, the Sultan would arrive accompanied by two of his favorites. After he was seated and all the other beauties of the Harem graced the scenery, they danced and offered the Sultan wine.

As he watched the lively and nicely covered bodies of the dancers, he would decide with who he was to spend the night. Then the other girls, who had been starving for male company, would start a game which the Sultan enjoyed.

Some of them would throw themselves at the Sultan's feet while others held back the lucky one. The Sultan, saving her from the hands of the hornies, would take her away to retire into the chamber of pleasure.

THE SULTAN WHO CHASED THE GIRLS IN THE HAREM'S TURKISH BATH

Sultan Selim II was very keen on hunting, attractive women, and parties which led him to his tragic end. His last Turkish Bath entertainment brought about his pathetic death.

It was one of the days when the Sultan felt like having a sex party in, the Turkish Bath of the Harem. The preparations started immediately.

The experienced women and the ones whom the Sultan had tasted before were not invited to this party and only the new and fresh girls were ordered to bathe the Sultan, and they waited for him naked.

When Selim II arrived at the hamam, he was already a little bit mellow. The humid and hot atmosphere of the hamam made him more slack.

Fresh and healthy naked virgins cleaned him thoroughly, and tenderly massaged his whole body all over. Then he played with them trying to catch the slippery bodies of the naked girls as they playfully ran away from him.

As his hands almost gripped a plump body, he stumbled and fell down on the marble floor. He was carried to his bed but all was too much for his exhausted heart.

14

Ersal Yavi, New cariyes in the Harem, Private Collection.

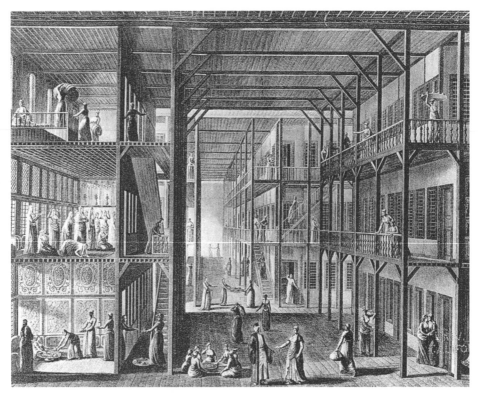

Topkapı Palace, Harem Section, M.Melling, 1819.

SULTAN MURAD III: THE SULTAN WHOSE CRAVING
FOR FLESH COULD NEVER BE FULFILLED

Murad III was also a pleasure-seeking Sultan. Historians have never been able to find out the exact number of his children, whose estimated number was between 106 and 130.

His age was also the golden age of the slave traders who sold the slave girls for the highest prices to the Palace.

The architecture and ornamentation of the pavilions which were built by his order as additional sections to the Harem of the Topkapı palace were exceptional.

The Sultan's favorite locations in the Palace where he spenthis moments of pleasure were Hünkâr Sofası and the pool at the basement of the Harem section.

Hünkâr Sofası was the place where the entertainment started. Musicians began to play in the afternoon and they went on until

Entertainment on the terrace Harem.

midnight. When the Sultan was turned on by the dances of the half-naked slave girls, he chose one of them for himself and the final scene of the entertainment took place either in his bedroom or on the marble floor of the Turkish Bath.

The Sultan sometimes sat on his throne by the pool and let the girls amuse him as they played around and bathed in the pool.

A favorite game began when the Kızlarağası placed a wooden perch over the pool! The girls with only a piece of scanty transparent cloth wrapped around their bodies climbed onto it playfully and when the Sultan wet them with cold water, they threw themselves into the pool pretending to drop the cloth around their bodies. Later, the most alluring one would be the guest of the Sultan's private party for two.

I ORDER YOU: BRING ME THE FATTEST WOMAN
OF THE WORLD

The only Ottoman Sultan who was reputed to be insane was Ibrahim II. He had been kept prisoner in his room until the day he ascended the throne. Long years of captivity and the fear of being strangled had impaired his sexual prowess but soon after he came to power, the physicians of the Palace cured him with aphrodisiacal plants and special pastes so that he could pursue young girls to his heart's content. He was never content with the women in his Harem and sent invitations even to the married women whom he heard about, and this caused the revolt of local administrations.

One day this crazy Sultan told his men to search for to the fattest woman of Istanbul. They looked everywhere and found a chubby Armenian who weighed 130 kilos. The Sultan who was very pleased with this woman called her 'Şivekar' and never favored the others. Her caresses became a shelter for his slight and feeble body. Perhaps he was cured of his psychosis when he got the feeling of being in her mother's womb. (His own mother, Kösem Sultan, was one of the most ruthless and authoritative characters in Ottoman history.)

Şivekar, who became his 6th Haseki, even got involved with state affairs.

It was rumored that the Valide Sultan who was Sultan Ibrahim II's mother, encouraged his avidity for forbidden fruit so that she could be the only ruler of the Empire and thus satisfy her main ambition.

Sultan Ibrahim II had his room in the Harem decorated with mirrors from top to toe and watched himself as he copulated with the girls.

Even the virgins who were regularly presented to him every Friday as a special delicacy could not gratify his appetite. He would sometimes demand all the women of the Harem in his room, and he would order them to walk around on their hands and knees pretending that they were the mares as he was the only stallion.

18

Sultan and his slave, Ersal Yavi, Private Collection.

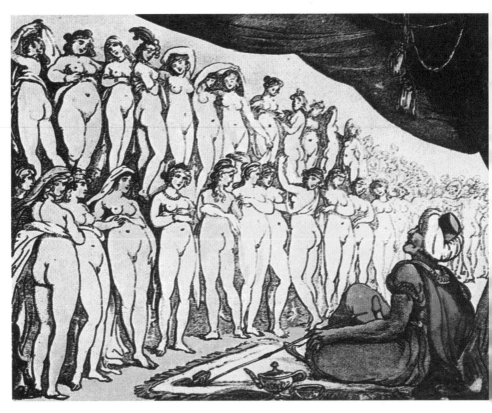

Thomas Rowlandson. An imagined Harem trough the eyes of a European.

EVEN THE SULTANS COULD FALL IN LOVE

Sultan Abdülhamid I who ruled the Ottoman Empire from 1774 to 1789, fell in love with one of the slave girls of his Harem at first sight.

Then he became the slave of the girl named Ruhşah who with her rather remote behavior became his instructor in genuine love.

One day Ruhşah resented her royal lover and decided to ignore him! The helpless and vulnerable Sultan thought of sending her away from the Harem, but he could not bear the idea of imagining her in somebody else's arms.

Here are the letters of the Sultan begging Ruhşah for love and forgiveness (The originals of these letters are secured at the library of the Topkapı Palace Museum):

1st. letter:

My Ruhşah,
Your Abdülhamid beseeches you...
Thy Lord, creator of all living things, has mercy and
forgiveness, but you doomed this loyal slave of yours,
me whose error was so petty.
I am on my knees, begging your pardon.
Please let me see you tonight; kill me if you wish,
I will surrender, but please do not disregard my cry, or I'll die.
I throw myself at your feet, I can no longer control myself.

Thomas Rowlandson. An imagined Harem trough the eyes of a European.

2nd. Letter:

My Lady,
Your Abdülhamid beseeches you.
Please, grant me the pleasure of your company,
That will be my joy.
Tonight is the night of the new moon.
I am in your hands. Please do me a kindness;
do not let me suffer anymore.
Last night I could hardly restrain myself.
I am your humble slave at your feet.

3rd. Letter:

Your Abdülhamid beseeches you.
What have I done? Human it is to err.
Please do not desert me because of a single misdeed.
May God curse me if I forsake you even
if your love ravages me. I am yours and you are mine,
we shall never part as long as the world goes round.
I am at your dainty feet, asking for your compassion.

Abdülhamid's letters must have moved his sweetheart. Ruhşah replaced Abdülhamid's first lady Ayşe later on and ruled his heart and treasury until the day she died.

THE SULTAN WHO WAS A WOMAN-HATER

Sultan Osman III who ascended the throne when he was 55 years old ruled the Ottoman Empire from 1754 to 1757.

In contrast to his successors and predecessors, he hated the gentle sex. Perhaps the source of his aversion for the opposite sex was his impotence. A history book states: "I wish that he is in the heaven of heavens now; respected Sultan Osman's resource of manhood was somehow indolent in producing the juice of fertility."

As soon as he rose to power, his first enforcement was to send away the singers and dancers of the Harem. He wore shoes with gold and silver nails to avoid the women at the Harem because

Sultan's favorite, J.J. A. Lecomt de Nouy, 1888.

they ran away panic-stricken when they heard his clattering shoes.

Sultan Osman III went out of the Palace three times a week to inspect what was going on in the city of Istanbul. On those days the women were ordered to stay at home behind the thick walls of the residences and they were not even allowed to dress up behind closed doors.

Although Sultan Osman III was the one and only Ottoman Sultan who never fancied women and spent his years of power in mating life difficult for the fair sex, he had two women at his side.

THE SULTAN'S FEAR OF THE RAGE OF WOMEN

Sultan Mustafa III who was the owner of the throne between the years 1757 and 1774, was very fond of Rifat Kadın whom he met in one of his outings.

Disregarding all the women of the Harem who were at his disposal at any time, he started an exclusive affair with her, meeting her in secret outside the Palace.

As time went by, this secret affair bored him and he wrote an order to the Grand Vizier to bring Rifat Kadın to the Palace covertly.

As soon as the Grand Vizier fulfilled his Sultan's order he received another letter which said:

> *My Vizier,*
> *Warn your wife and daughter to keep their lips sealed when*
> *they are asked about my Rifat. Her presence in*
> *the Palace should be a complete secret.*
> *Use the side door of the garden to let her in but never*
> *direct her to the main door which is full of Harem guards.*
> *Beware of inquisitors, and be dumb.*

Why the Royal rascal was so very cautious of the birds in the cage, we do not know, because there has never been a case like his before in the history of the Ottoman Sultans. Perhaps the ruler of the grand Empire was wise enough to stay away from the fury of the jealous females.

A woman, Levni, 18th century

Rifat Kadın lived in the Grand Vizier's house and was admitted to the Palace with difficulty. Mustafa III had the courage, to announce her as his fourth legal wife after a long time.

ANGELS OF THE CRYSTAL BALL

The first half of the 17th century was the age of reforms and modernizes under the leadership of Ahmet III who was the dynast of the Ottoman Empire for 27 years starting with the year 1703. His era is also known as the Tulip Age (Lâle Devri). At that time a rare tulip bulb used to cost a fortune.

Ahmet III was also a man of carnal pleasures. He spent his days enjoying himself at the festivities organized at the Hünkâr Sofası which was the largest room in the Harem.

Well-known and talented lady musicians played his favorite Limes as the dancing girls sang and danced. Sipping his wine on his throne he gazed at the most beautiful girls of all breeds as they played around. What he relished most was watching those girls as they jumped and tried to catch a crystal ball hanging down from the high ceiling.

The display of the newly blossomed flesh of the charming girls who competed with each other joyously made him sigh, and he could not help chasing the half-naked girls. This game went on until the Sultan got them in the Hünkâr bath.

Portrait of Mihrimah Sultan. 18th century, from the J.Amram collection.

THE SULTAN WHO HUNTED THE LOVERS
AT THE HAREM

The Harem was so strictly protected from the male eyes that not even a male fly could enter it. The girls who desperately starved for male company were sometimes even willing to have an affair with a castrated black eunuch, and some letters written by the captives of the golden cage are proof of lesbian relationships

Portrait of Gülnuş Sultan. 19th century, from the Topkapı Palace Museum.

among them. A slave girl who dared to get involved with a male servant from the Enderun section of the Palace was doomed to death. But if they were fearless enough to love each other and risk their lives such lovers can only win our love and respect.

Here is the legendary story of a slave girl and a boy from the Enderun: Once upon a time there was a very handsome boy whose name was Mehmet. One day his eyes met the eyes of an ange-

Harem. Jean-Baptiste Van Mour, from the Azize Taylan collection.

lic and pretty girl in front of the gate of the aviary. He should not
have looked at her eyes and hands and bend his head down as
the was ordered but he could not help witnessing her beauty and
his heart began to pound.

The slave girl was also attracted by his charm. So they fell in love with each other.

28

The interior door of the Harem became their love nest where they secretly met and made love. When the Sultan was informed about this forbidden affair, he could not believe his ears but kept an eye on the slave girl.

One night when Mehmet and his sweetheart were in each other's arms, they saw a glittering dagger in the hand of a shadow approaching them, and they caught a glimpse of the Sultan in the darkness of the night. They ran away in panic and were chased by the Sovereign himself.

When they came to a courtyard, the Sultan lost sight of the lovers. There were cupboards in the courtyard and the Sultan saw a piece of cloth hanging down from the cover of the cupboard. He held up his dagger and removed the cover. In astonishment, he saw that there was no one there. He decided then that the lovers were sanctified and had disappeared. He stood still in front of the cupboard and saluted them. A golden lock was put on the cupboard by him later so that the lovers would not be disturbed.

The daughter of Sultan Ibrahim (1640-1646), Fatma Sultan, became the wife of the second vizier Yusuf Paşa when she was three years old. A year later, the vizier was killed by the Sultan and the poor child was a widow at the age of four. The same year, she married Admiral Fazıl Paşa with a lavish wedding; however, her husband was sent to a mission abroad and she was doomed to loneliness. When she reached sixteen, Fazıl Paşa died and she was a widow again.

There is no record of her having been in the bridal chamber.

Sultan Ahmed its daughter Ayşe Sultan was seven years old when her wedding ceremony was held. She had two husbands during her childhood.

Ayşe Sultan, who had a number of husbands because of political assassinations, lived a nuptial night only with her fourth husband.

Sultan Ahmed its second daughter, Fatma Sultan, is known as the Lady Sultan who had the highest number of legitimate husbands. She had wedding ceremonies with 12 different men all of whom were viziers.

A casual day in Harem. Thomas Allom.

IS BEING CASTRATED A STONE IN LOVE'S PATH

It is believed that when a man is castrated his sexual attraction to women vanishes, but it is also a fact that the genital organs of boys who were castrated at a very young age mature, and that the sexual desire for the opposite sex awakens gradually.

Even though all the castrated boys were examined by the physician of the Sultan carefully, there are some documents on their secret relationships to the slave girls in the Harem.

One of these documents was written by a fireman who spent most of his life at the Palace.

Here is an excerpt from his manuscript:

"I swear that those black betrayers have a relationship to one or two slave girls; whatever they earn, they spend on them, and they make love at every occasion they have.

They are said to be freed from their lustful senses, but then; how do they make sex? These filthy black misbelievers are all robust.

They are the customers of the slave traders and hide at least one or two girls in their rooms. There is a great rivalry among them and their eyes are all green when it comes to their lovers.

I have worked for 18 years in the Old Palace and I am familiar with the core of this matter. I even taught the science of the Koran to some of these black creatures and it really worked. They turned into tamed horses, so I had a chance to learn what the devil was going on within the Harem walls.

Beware of these corrupted black unbelievers your Eminence, their loyalty is a lie and they shall never be trusted.

These perfidious creatures are the sons of the bitches who can never stay away from malice, and they never marry a decent woman, and copulate like stray dogs.

Do women get the same taste as a healthy man does from these black eunuchs? If you are curious let me tell you: Yes, and maybe they get more than that.

I had two partners at work and both of them married the slavegirls who were dismissed from the Harem. After a week of their marriage, they had to divorce them because their wives were bold enough to say that the black eunuchs were much better in bed."

Now, let's go into the intimacy of a black eunuch and read his sincere confessions:

"It was one of those days when I was more tired than usual. I fell asleep as soon as I lay on my bed. In my sleep, I felt a sweet thrill as if an invisible hand was stimulating every single point on my body. I woke up and that foamy feeling increased; I was not able to understand what it was but it gave me great pleasure.

As this situation held on, my great enchantment turned into a feeling of disturbance because in the morning of such nights I woke up like a wreck.

Seeking sympathy, I decided to pour out my grief to one of my close friends but in the middle of our chat he burst into laughter as if I had told him the funniest story. This led me to an even deeper depression.

Then I realized that this obscure situation was just a revolt of my manhood, brutally persecuted by ferocious hands.

This salacious feeling took hold of me and got even worse as I was always surrounded by the most beautiful women of the world who were very easy in manners without paying any attention to my presence. I could hardly control myself not to sail into their lips, tits and arms. Then I understood that I was searching for lust and not love.

There were a lot of sexy girls at the Palace with whom I could realize my will but such an affair might have ended in the shear legs, so I decided to get married. We have been together for long years but I have never asked my wife why she has married me. You know, when you hear the bitter reality from somebody else it hurts more. She is a loyal woman and she is always eager to fulfill the duties of a wife. I sometimes have a feeling that I get more than a complete man. But it is poor me who will always live with this deficiency."

PERFORMING THE OLDEST PROFESSION OF THE WORLD WITHIN THE BORDERS OF THE OTTOMAN EMPIRE

Although Islam preached a strict moral code, the women were confined to homely life, and the Ottoman male could marry four women and buy as many slaves as he could attired, the so-called oldest profession of the world was fully practiced within the Otto-man borders as well.

Laws and legislations against adultery put to power by Yavuz Sultan Selim in 1512 stated that:

"If the offender is a married man and is caught in the very act, he shall pay 400 silver coins. If the man is of the middle class, his fine is reduced to 300 silver coins. The fine is 200 silver coins for a poorer fellow and 100 silver coins for the impoverished."

The fine of adultery for bachelors was more moderate; 100 silver coins from the rich one, 50 silver coins from the lower in-come group and 30 silver coins from the poor. If women committed adultery, their husbands were obliged to pay their fine.

"If a slave girl does prostitution, the fine is half the amount of the fine for a free person."

Even Yavuz Sultan Selim's standing orders are the substantiation of widespread adultery and prostitution and they provided a huge sum of income for the treasury of the state.

Prostitutes were registered first in 1565. According to the related documents, the inhabitants of the Sultangir neighborhood on the coast of the Goldenhorn, informed the Muslim Judge (Kadı) against five women. They claimed that these women ran a brothel and that Arab Fati was the matron of Narin, Kamer and Yümni from Balat and Nefise from Crete. The Kadı decided to seize their property and banish the harlots whose names indicate that they were Muslim

The only option left for the women who were sent away from Istanbul because of prostitution was to join a Chengi (female dancer) group and stroll about Anatolia. Usually the Chengi le-

An Elegant lady's promenade in Istanbul, 19th century.

ader built up tents in the outskirts of the towns in the evenings. If they were invited to a residence; they would usually go wearing men's clothes and attend the party.

Sultan Selim II was also in favor of the banishment of these naughty women but as far as we gather, nothing put an end to the sweet bargain. Even the officials who were in charge of maintaining public order and security could not help falling into the trap of their dexterous bodies.

As the prohibitions of Sultan Selim II were precisely executed, there appeared a lot of laundries where the customers were usually young unmarried men. Professional women who could not find shelter in the neighborhoods found the remedy in having two jobs. They washed the sweat-smelling clothes of the young and muscular men during the day and in the darkness of the night, they found the cure to their "illness" on the hairy chests of these love-seekers in the back rooms of the laundry. Unfortunately, the real function of these places was discovered, and they too were banned.

In the 16th century, prostitution nested in the harbor of Istanbul. Housing the mosques and tombs of Islamic forefathers, Eyüp was a reputed religious quarter and therefore this reputation and the crowded population of Eyüp provided good shelter for the pimps and the concubines.

Husbands who were absolutely sure of their decent wives' faithfulness never hesitated to let them leave their houses to go to Eyüp, so that they would pay religious services. However, their wives met their lovers in the gloomy dessert shops along with the prostitutes who bargained with their customers.

A decree prohibited women to enter the dessert shops of Eyüp in 1573. Then the ingenious young lovers and the flesh-sellers found the solution in meeting in boats. After having a good time at the deserted coasts, they used to return to the harbour. The state ordered the boatmen not to rent boats to young couples in 1580.

None of these precautions sufficed to prevent the oldest profession of the world. The Imams of every neighborhood were authorized to report frivolous inhabitants and to organize raids to any house under suspicion, but the flagrant offence was not punished if the man accepted to marry the guilty woman.

In the meantime, agents did not remain inactive and informed the Imams on the red-lantern houses (brothel) of the neighborhood.

One day the Imam of Imrahor received a letter which read as follows:

"I declare that the dwellers of the house next to clerk Little Hafız's house, that is, brothel-keeper Ayşe Hanım and her illegitimate husband should leave this neighborhood within a week. This neigh-

A couple caught making love on the river bank. 18th century miniature.

borhood wilt never has any peace unless they go away.

Today I saw a couple of rakes and whores entering their house and on Monday three tramps and three Armenian bitches visited them. I have also seen a lot of tramps around that house. "

Slave traders also contributed a lot to this market. Slaves were displayed and sold at the open air markets before the slave bazaar was established. The customers used this opportunity to contact the girls, and if they could come to terms with the dealers, hired them out for the night. Sometimes, purchasers wished to test the goods and the trader let them keep the girl for a short period of time and got his share.

A raid to forbidden love by the inhabitants of the neighborhood.
Miniature from Zenannâme, 18th century. İ.Ü.Library

Cariyes in the Harem. Dolmabahçe Palace Museum

The foreign visitors of Istanbul also abused the advantage of this commerce by renting the girls at frequent intervals. When this was noticed by-the officials, all the slaves were paid for and taken away from the foreigners and the traders were punished.

In his famous book of travels, Evliya Çelebi mentioned that there were pimps among businessmen, and even gave their number to be exactly 212, and wrote that some of these traders were buggers.

Sultan Murad IV (1623-1640), who was against any addiction, took strict precautions to grip the increase of prostitution during his reign.

Historians refer to Sultan Mustafa II (1695-1703), Sultan Ahmet III (1703-1730) and Sultan Selim III (1789-1803) as the Sultans who had a predilection to escape strict Islamic rules. During the Tulip Era under Sultan Ahmed III, women were allowed to jo-

Women of Istanbul. Amadeo Preziosi.

in the festivities in Kağıhane wearing their thin silk garments; however, the catchy figures of the ladies under the silk covers set many a man on fire and the secret flirtation of the sexes was condemned by the community. So the Sultan had to command women to dress up in a decent way. To my surprise, the Ottoman Sultans were all prosecutors of ladies' outfits even at times of modernization. Women were warned about thin and tight clothes which could arouse sexually and stimulate men, and the attractiveness of the gentle sex was always associated with carnal desire. Sultan Selim III abrogated thin outdoor coats. He also threatened the tailors with execution on the gallows in front of their shops if they were to break the rules on ladies' clothing.

In 1752, the rumors about young women who fooled around in the outskirts of Istanbul, Çamlıca, Sarıyer and Beykoz (in Bosphorus) instigated another decree which ordered those female

An entertaintment with beauties at Kağıthane - İstanbul. Münif Fehim.

A rascal's night of joy. Ibrahim Safi.

rascals to watch their step. Prostitution cases recorded in the documents were mostly from Istanbul and only some rare instances
from Anatolia were considered. It is also a fact that such a profession could only be profitable in the areas where trade and opu-

lence substantiated the means for it.

In the 19th century, the Galata and Beyoğlu regions of Istanbul where the majority of non-Muslim lived and the nightly entertainment flourished, were the red lantern districts of the city.

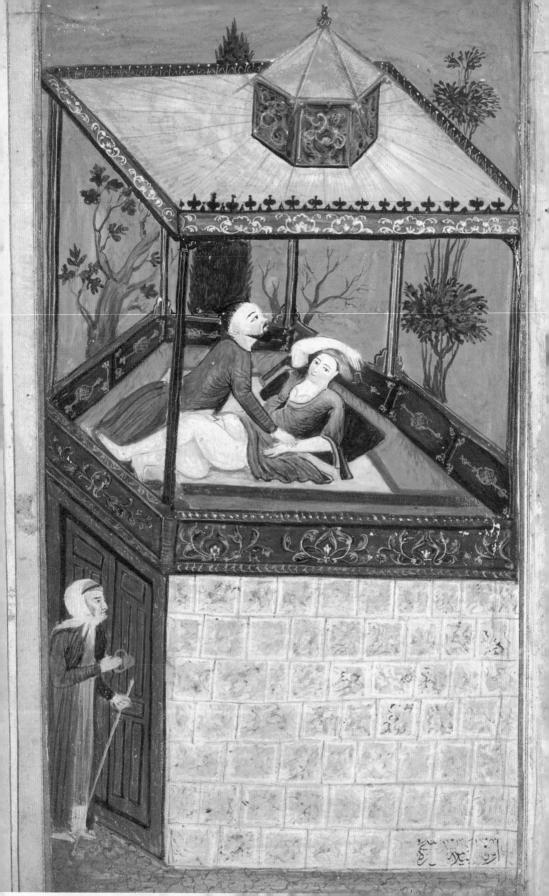

A picnic in the meadows.

The brothels of Istanbul were mentioned in the travel book with the title, "*Guide des Voyageurs en Allemagne, en Hongrie et a Constantinople*" and which was published in Germany in 1811. The author of the travel book, Reichardt wrote that almost all the girls working in the brothels were Jewish, and that besides the professionals there were also older women who sought satisfaction or women who wished to take revenge on their husbands for neglecting them. Just as Reichardt was writing about the streetwalkers of Istanbul a hundred years ago, researcher Olivier portrayed some other coquettes who fished for customers: "Young Greek boys in women's clothes and with coquettish air who were

A copulating couple on the terrace and an old woman peeping.
Miniature from Hamse-i Atai. T.İ.E.M. Library

45

after clients occupied the streets of Istanbul without any hindrance. In contrast to the Turkish guys, Greek boys had long hair which they combed carefully with oriental scents and decorated with flowers, and they put on make-up on their cheeks, eyebrows and eyelashes."

The era of Sultan Mahmud II (1808-1839) brought some liberty to women. By courtesy of the Sultan, even the members of the Harem could promenade in the outskirts of Istanbul in their colorful and shiny silk coats. Men or women who chased the forbidden fruit started to have more air to breathe. But Beyoğlu preserved its fame as being the focal point of recreation in Istanbul where you could hear many different dialects of various languages uttering words of the universal lingo.

In 1860, a new brothel started to offer services to the public in Aksaray as an alternative to the bordellos of Beyoğlu. The owner was an Irish woman so this new house of pleasure was famed as The House of the Outlander' which later initiated the establishment of others where the talented artisans were Muslim Turks, Armenians and Greek women. However, Beyoğlu always remained the prominent center of amusement and love. Shehzades (Sons of the Sultans), Pashas and other eminent members of the Palace joined the crew of hunters in Beyoğlu during the age of Sultan Abdülhamid II (1876-1908), and the prey of these royal hunters were the stars of the European show troupes.

The arrival of the White Russians who escaped from the communist regime at the beginning of the 20th century added some more color and joy to Beyoğlu, and the love trade flourished. These- were the years when the number of Turkish whores made up one third of the registered prostitutes in Istanbul.

After the foundation of the Turkish Republic by Atatürk (1923), women were granted their full rights, and some decrease in prostitution as well as sexual deviations could be observed.

46

ENCYCLOPAEDIA OF SEXOLOGY
(BAHNAME)

The "Bahnâmes" were written to instruct people in sex and eroticism, and they have a long history in eastern cultures.

The Indian "*Kama Sutra*" and the Arabian "*Perfumed Garden*" are only two of the well known examples of this type of books.

After the 15th century, the Ottomans were able to profit from these books. These books which were decorated with miniatures created by highly talented artists, gave recipes for aphrodisiacs, sexual health, and contraceptive methods, as well as positions during intercourse which allowed both sexes more satisfaction.

There were exclusive miniatures in the" books of joy presented to the Palace, whereas the public editions were a lot more modest. The Bahnâmes written in the 18th and 19th centuries were mostly on sexual techniques and erotic fantasies. The ones which were published in Istanbul were sold covertly in bookstores.

The rich could pay huge amounts of money to get one illustrated in rich colors but there were books without pictures for those of modest means. However, they could always purchase the pictures later and improve their lovemaking techniques.

Now, if I have aroused your desire to learn about what was going on between the Ottoman male and his lovers in those days, let us climb up the plane tree as old as Methuselah with our binoculars and start peeping.

EXCERPTS FROM A BAHNAME ON SEXUAL POSITIONS
"She lies on her back, puts her hands under her head and with legs wide apart, pulls her knees towards her chest. He comes and holds her, they are now face to face and with his chest touching her nipples, he knocks at the door of her pussy with his stiff penis; by moving her buttocks slowly up, she takes him in and as she moves more swiftly they both reach the climax."

She lies on her back with one leg up. Her hot companion settles down between her legs, and makes his cock touch the lips of

47

her cunt. They both enjoy the thrilling moments of pause, and then she gets giddy and says ' My love, my patience is exhausted because of my desire for you, I beg you, please be gentle with me'. As he has his way with her, she holds him very tight and the story ends happily."

"The couple sits on the bed very close to each other with their feet underneath them. He uses his hands to put his organ in her and they move closer and closer.

This position needs a very lengthy penis.

She lies on her back in anticipation and holds her legs up. When she feels her man, she grasps him with her legs vigorously. He moves into her holding her shoulders and harmonious motions bring them to satisfaction."

"She stands up with her hands on her belly. The man dives in like a wild horse. "Oh! My darling you have ravaged my cunt," she says coyly. He doesn't stop screwing her of course, on the contrary he moves faster until she is done."

"She lies down on her right side with her legs stretched. He gets behind her and places one of his thighs on her and the other one between her legs. He wets his cock with his saliva and starts rubbing it on her vagina and asshole. When he reaches the point of ejaculation, he pushes it into the nearest hole speedily. However, anal intercourse is wicked and so, he should save his semen for the proper place."

"With her face down, she pulls one of her knees to her chest and heaves herself up on her feet. He inserts his massive engine in her and listens to her moans of delight. As he comes, he pulls her closer by holding her hair and increases his speed until his final ejaculation of sperm triggers off. This position gives amazing pleasure to the couple."

"She waits for her man in a stooped position. When he is there, her ass starts dancing and she sucks him very deep into her. This position is very convenient for an unexpected quick flight with a slave girl, and if the man is strong enough it can be delectable.

"She dresses up as if she is going out and leans against a wall.

A couple making love. From an oriental Bahnâme, İ.Ü.Library

48

بستند و بنا و عروسی و میش کرد و منکر رسم و آیین پریان است بجا آوردند و دو
سوخته فراق کشیده بعد از رنج به کام دل رسیدند و کام دل از یکدیگر گرفتند که چه خوش باشد
که بعد از رنج بسیار، رسند بر سر گنج و کام دل و دلدار، القصه تا چهل شبانه روز گذشت

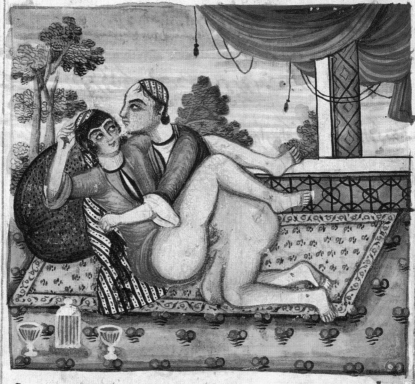

کردند و یک سال آنجا بودند بعد از آن پسری شد و کفت این شاهزاده اکبر اینشهر پدر و مادر
فرستم مرا پیغ صوابی باشد کفت پدر و مادر می دانش یکدیگر شاد کفت هر چند دنیای آتش
آمد بیقرار رفتن تا شاهزاده زبان ادب بوسیده و شاه زاد کفت پس سهیل
در کار از زیاش شاهزاده بسیار کوشیده در زیر و جواهر الخرد در گلستن ارم بهم میرسید
بار کردند و روانه شد چون مع الجلال بشهر سرندیب رسیدند دیه کردند ملک

The man comes, takes off her veil and kisses her and then tears her "şalvar" (pants with baggy legs) off from one of her legs and hold her naked leg up. The view of her cunt arouses him and he screws her wildly, as she shrieks with excitement.

THOSE PARTS OF YOUR MISTRESS THAT ARE
TO BE KISSED

For your information, a woman's cheeks, lips, eyes, forehead, neck, breasts, and navel area are the parts you should kiss. If the outer lips of her pussy are clean and pure they are also delicious, of course, if you wish. You can never have enough of kissing her.

A MEDICINE TO PREVENT PREGNANCY

Rezaki grapes are crushed in their own juice and mixed thoroughly. Then a bit of musk root is added to this mixture and the woman's vagina should be cleaned with a very clean piece of cloth soaked in this medicine before intercourse. This makes her like a virgin and she doesn't get pregnant.

A Bahnâme manuscript at the end of the 19th century.

ما سندك دعيزلنده ايرلك سنت سكن جلديني زمانج راهم Marie هنز ياغمه ؟؟؟
نلج وقته قاده مساعد اونيه يه كوجيول جلك كزنك تابك أرياتكز محفلريه دلسو دُ عماركونك كيذ
اعنده ببلرو دعرب نياقه سنترم غريبالمسو ؛ مورشدى .
نياعمه جيرين ببالره نونن قوبه اورشن . باجا عنكش بنى قاريونك بانده ما اسلكم ره ؛ السيرك دمُ
بوشكسه .... سنته سكر برمونى جلاوزنده كوزلري آجيف . بعاونك اوزوده اوزوم لرينه . بوركه وُسنايرو فه
نعف بحمد كزاليلم بر سنت دو شنما . بو صباح اونك علقم بر بانتقلمه واردك . بيجكر اينك دفه كوردبه
برمفياد جماع اون نمدى شهونك طباق بوطوا اينه عاديشه . رؤيا سنك ارقا آنما نديى عفعه ؟؟ره ؛ ؛
نليلى نميده قاده نراو اير انكز كتابك محفلرنمذُ عيالاره دُ نزده تنراء كوبلره اوبانفكم كنعا كنه
باينه دونتره بكره مومدى .

Another page from the Bahnâme manuscript at the end of the 19th century.
From the collection of the author.

THE GORGEOUS WOMEN OF ISTANBUL

In 1784, a famous poet of his age, Enderunlu Fazıl Bey who reveled in his homosexuality and his spectacular personality, wrote a book on the most captivating men and women of the world when he was convinced by one of his lovers. I would like to give you some examples of the sections where he described the fair sex of Istanbul in his book.

"Istanbul which is a unique and divine city shines gloriously in the world. God has gifted all the women and men of Istanbul with loveliness and charm. They all have rose-pink complexions. The way they walk is admired by everyone in the world but their characters are widely different from each other. Let me tell you about them and let us explore the devils and the angels."

THE FIRST GROUP OF ISTANBUL WOMEN

They always live behind the curtains and even the worst disaster can not make them leave their hiding places. These ladies love their homes more than anything else. They are like rubies framed with silver; they are roses in a vase and parrots in a cage. Their hair which gently falls on their forehead has not been brushed by the morning breeze and their tender skin has not been touched by the sun yet.

THE SECOND GROUP OF ISTANBUL WOMEN

Even if they look decent, all of them are of easy virtues. Their costumes are colorful. The rich purple of their outdoor mantle can easily divert you. If they intentionally dress up to enhance their beauty, that means they are out for hunting men.

They wander in the shopping district pretending to look for something with a couple of slaves attending them. They go into the shops with a coquettish air to seduce the shopkeeper they cast their veiled look on. Then a meaningful conversation starts between them. The woman asks coyly: "Have you got anything for me? Let me have a look at it if it is good enough." These words are a discreet cipher between them. Then her beautiful face

داش بانونك طوير يدر

A lady from Istanbul, Levni, 1725. Topkapı Palace Museum.

Women of Istanbul in Kağıthane. Miniature from Zenannâme. 18th century.

behind her transparent veil and her fingers decorated with henna hunt him like a hawk, and she takes him to her house. Her husband has gone to work early in the morning to earn money, and he does not have the slightest idea about what is going on in his house when he is away.

THE THIRD GROUP OF ISTANBUL WOMEN:

These women are always at the market. Their slanted and heavily made up eyes gaze amorously on their gentle faces. How-

54

ever, this can be deceptive because some of them are quite shrewish. When they go to the "hamam" (Turkish Bath), they take loads of beautifying cosmetics with them and hope to recover the fresh bloom of their youth. There is also rivalry between these prostitutes and they look forward to having a fight and insult each other wherever they meet.

THE FOURTH GROUP OF ISTANBUL WOMEN:
This is the group of lesbians who have appeared lately in Istanbul. They didn't exist in the good old days. They fall in love

Two young ladies from Istanbul.

with each other and they even use artifice to get what they want during their relationship. They use an artificial organ. I am embarrassed to mention its name myself but it is called 'Zıbık'.

Lesbians are well-educated, polite and even tempered. They devote themselves to their lovers and never deceive them. Their speech is sophisticated when they compliment each other like; "My beauty, rose bouquet, my pearl, here I am", "My silver colored love, I have been longing for you", "My rose bud, my zealous lady, let me die at your feet."

This is how the amorous moments start.

I have thought very hard to find out why women fancy each other as sex partners and I think I know the answer. Women who have had sex with a number of men become satiated and bored with the male organ and so they start being charmed by ladies. Once in a while when they happen to see an irresistible youth they don't mind breaking the rule though.

Anyway, this is a dilemma. Let us leave them alone.

A lady from Istanbul in her autdoor mantle, Levni, 1725.
Topkapı Palace Museum.

A voman in the Turkish Bath. Abdullah Buhari, 1742. Topkapı Palace Museum.

THE AESTHETIC NORMS
OF THE OTTOMAN MAN

The Ottoman Empire ruled over the vast lands in Anatolia, the Balkan Peninsula, Greece, Austria, Hungary, Egypt, Palestine, North Africa, the Aegean Islands and the coasts of the Black Sea and the Mediterranean in the 16th century.

Istanbul was the capital and as we mentioned before, the men who lived there did not burden themselves with the concept of race discrimination. Therefore the selected top beauties from all of these countries found themselves in the wealthiest houses, in Konaks or even at the Palace and lived in prosperity. This wide variety of girls from all over the world gave the Ottoman gentlemen the opportunity to observe the differences in their physical nature, and develop guidelines on the most desirable characteristics for sexual satisfaction.

Sophistication led the way to new tastes and diversions, and refined the criteria of beauty.

The Ottoman connoisseurs of the fair sex fancied plump, pearl-complexioned, made up and perfumed women of medium height above all. If their hands and feet were ornamented with henna (a reddish-brown dye extracted from the leaves of fragrant flowers), if all the extra hair on the body were waxed off, particularly after a long Turkish bath session, and if the thoroughly freshened ladies blushed and mellowed because of hot vapor, so much the better.

Now let us have a look at the formulated criteria of the connoisseurs of the biological drive.

The magic number of this formula was four:

The four mysterious blacks : Hair, eyebrows, eye lashes, and the color of the eyes.
The four enigmatic cinnabar-reds : Tongue, lips, cheeks, and jowls.

Naked Odalisk, Eugene Guérard.

The four round beauties : Face, eyes, wrists and heels.
The four lengthy goods   : Neck, nose, eyebrows and fingers.
The four sweet-smelling charms : Nose, hands and feet,
                                                 armpits and vagina.
The four wide deceivers :   Forehead, eyes, tits and buttocks.
The four narrow secrets :   Nostrils, ear holes, navel cave and
                                              vagina.
The four small appetizers : Mouth, lips, hands and feet, ears.

Hard-working and very fastidious connoisseurs expanded this
list with some 'musts' as follows:
Head: neither big nor small
Height: neither tall nor short
Should neither be overweight nor underweight and must

60

have very luxuriant hair.

And the most important 'must' was her smile and her light-heartedness. Zest should joyfully be reflected by her smile and she should call him to the heaven of devotion in silence.

What about the indications of a lascivious woman? Again the criteria were formed through worldly experience. Here is the list for you in case you should wish to benefit from this treasure:

- Big mouth; wide vagina.
- Small mouth; tight vagina.
- Full lower lip; outer lips of her vulva are thick.
- Thin upper lip; outer lips of the vulva are also thin and soft.
- Thin lower lip; her vaginal entrance doesn't get wet easily.
- Top of the tongue like dried currants; cold vagina.
- Nose like a bottle; doesn't enjoy intercourse.
- Thin hair; lumpy vagina.
- Long chin; big clitoris.
- A big, fat and oval face; big and tight vulva and small arse.
- Fat feet; sizable and fertile womb and a very big vagina.
- Fleshy and strong thighs; has a lot of bodily appetite and can't live without mating.
- Thin lips, small and conic breasts; is not keen on love making but if you work on her you can improve her libido.
- Blue-eyed and ruddy-complexioned; there is no hope.
- Always cheerful and active; she longs for love.
- Enjoys dancing all the time; she is tempted to be in your arms.

Turkish men still have the habit of studying women. I suppose because of their desire to fish for these "secret" indications.

GIRLS TO ENJOY (ODALISKS)

The Ottoman male had the privilege to have four wives. He also had the luxury of having mistresses. Some higher officials, the distinguished members of society, and the rich bought girls for their lustful satisfaction.

Pleasure girls could be bought at the slave bazaars or from the merchants who flourished by this trade. Such maids from Europe, the Mediterranean, the Caucasus, Africa, Russia and Arabia were always on demand, depending on their beauty and supply. They were bought and sold like any other good on the market.

There were no legal brothels in the Empire until the end of the 19th century. Prostitution was done in secret and its punishment was especially severe for women. No neighborhood wanted to house brothels and there was always the danger of being raid-

Odalisk and slave. J.-A. Dominique Ingres, 1842.

ed. Nevertheless Ottoman men relished having different partners. Wedlock with four wives was O.K. but never enough for them. Besides those whose wives had gotten old, fat or ill felt that they needed younger and better women. There was no problem for wealthy men since they could buy as many pleasure girls as their purses allowed. They generally chose white slave girls between the ages of fifteen and twenty. Distinguished people went to the houses where the girls were sold personally but in disguise, preferring to select the girl of their taste themselves.

The slave master brought the almost naked girls into the room one by one. The ones who appealed to their fancy were paid for and sent to the Konaks.

There was no enforcement though. The girls could refuse the customer if they wanted to. They had to consent before' the payment was made. Naturally this practice sometimes led to an increase of price. The mediator and the girl sometimes refused the eager customer upon their private agreement, so that he would

Odalisk. Private Collection.

The Slave Market. Jéan Leon Gérôme.

offer more money for the girl.

Moreover, wealthy men were also interested in very young teenagers. These tender girls were thoroughly trained by the retired women of the trade. When they got to be fifteen or sixteen years old, they started their career in the world of passion.

Don't ever think that anything you have read above could be realized if the permission of the eminent lady of the house was not taken. Anything contrary to her will might have ended up by being returned to the slave bazaar. Ottoman men knew a lot of ways to persuade their legal wives in order to keep a girl they fancied. They even offered them to exchange their object of carnal delight.

The main concerns of the wealthy Ottoman men were watching their Venuses have fun in the pool, thinking about which one to choose for the night, and getting carried away with sensual pleasure.

Pleasure girls were graded higher than the other slave girls in the household. They had their own rooms and could spend as much as they wanted on clothing.

Some esteemed statesmen owned so many girls that they could compete with the Sultan in this respect.

The Sultans who were addicted to women like Mahmud II also used these girls as a means of corruption. Mahmud II offered beautiful girls to the high rank officials in his entourage in order to have them in his grip. This was another factor for the cost of such maids to be so high. And the merchants got richer and richer. It was rumored that there were some merchants who lived happily ever after on the money they got from a single slave.

Ramiz Paşa, the Commander of the fleet in 1808, was also a man of carnal desires. One day he heard about a woman whose name was Hatayi, and that she was reputed to remain a virgin after making love no matter how often and with whom. He became obsessed with her. He got in touch with almost all the slave masters and granted them a lot of gold to get her. Unfortunately there is no record of his probable victory.

Dark beauties from Arabia or Ethiopia were also favored by some adventurous ecstasy-seekers but there were none at the Court until the reign of Sultan Ahmet I. He happened to grac his

The Slave Market. Thomas Allom, 1845.

Harem with one of these curly-haired charmers. What happened to her? She didn't wake up one morning; she was strangled by jealous white hands.

As anyone can imagine, birth control was a crucial issue. It was forbidden for the pleasure girls to get pregnant and if by any mischance they did get pregnant, there were some ways of abortion for help. Usually a kind-hearted master couldn't bear the idea of having the baby aborted and that meant the promotion of the pleasure girl to the status of a legal wife after the child was born.

The Ottoman Empire had vast territories. Governors of distant provinces like Benghazi, Arabia, Tripoli, and Yemen chose mistresses from the native population. They even sent remarkable gifts to Istanbul for the authorities at home.

Racism never cast its ugly shadow over the pleasures of the Ottoman men; there was no discrimination of race, color, language or religion for them.

The only criterion concerning the pleasures of the flesh was beauty alone. Naturally if the gentleman had enough bucks.

The Slave Market. Giulio Rosati, Private Collection.

Dancing Chengi, Levni. 172, from Topkapı Palace Museum.

DANCING GIRLS (CHENGIS)

"Raks", an oriental dance, is an outstanding form of entertainment for the Muslim society. It is such a symbol that it has been accepted to be a characteristic of eastern cultures worldwide.

Ottomans also enjoyed this art of musical entertainment combined with dance. "

In the past, people who wanted to be professional dancers got together and formed groups. Some of these groups consisted of male dancers, the Köcheks, and the other ones composed of female dancers were named 'troupe of dancing girls'. There were no mixed groups. Individual dancers were called "Chengi". The troupes of dancing girls performed only for women and they were more or less like stage actresses. They had a leader, assistants of the leader, 12 dancers and 4 women playing the string instruments called "saz".

The leader was usually an experienced woman, most probably a lesbian who had spent her life in troupes. Her house was almost an academy for future group leaders. If there was a house from which the joyful sound of music poured out, it meant that the most well-formed, charming and frivolous girls were being trained at that place.

Young and handsome guys and old rascals with a lot of cash were equally attracted to these houses and spent most of their time in such neighborhoods. But alas! Life would not be easy because the general inclination of the Chengis was not for men but for their own sex, for women with lips of fire and ivory complexions.

Frankly, the Chengis had the reputation of being the well-known lesbian group of the Ottoman society.

If there was a to be wedding, which meant several days full of various festivities, troupes could be engaged after a hard bargain with the group leader. The group stayed in the house of the host throughout the wedding and entertained the guests.

The arrival of the troupe was always a phenomenon. Men gazed raptly at these seductive beauties and their lovely bodies

A Chengi. Van Moor. Engraving, 1720.

covered with colorful clothes. The suggestive words and the bawdy messages they exchanged along the way went on until the troupe arrived at the place they were going to perform. Their rooms were reserved in the Harem section of these houses; the residents and other guests were forbidden to enter these rooms, though the lively voice of the dancers preparing for the show always incited the curiosity of the female members of the household. The ladies of the household spent most of their time eavesdropping at the doors and even forced their way in to see what was going on.

Tension increased as the audience waited for the chengis. They let go of their curly long hair which glittered on the stage. They moved their bodies in fine transparent garments and gold threaded skirts and in embroidered vests and laces which were designed to show off their tits with the rhythm of the music. With the cymbals at their fingers, they moved their shoulders, swirled their bellies and twisted their buttocks while the music played mischievously. They held the guests spellbound with their enchanting sensual dance.

Sometimes they changed their costumes and stepped on the stage as seductive young men. This was known to be the best part of the show because the ladies in the audience waited for them with aching hearts.

They displayed their interest in the Chengis either by covered or by straightforward remarks.

Most of the Chengis had lovers among the wealthy women and middle-aged widows. During the show, Chengis smiled at them and sent secret messages with their gestures.

Rich women were always the center of special attention for the Chengis. They exploited this chance to establish intimate relationships with the eligible ladies among the crowd. It was customary to attach gold coins on Chengis' bodies, which was an opportunity to exchange murmured invitations and messages.

The rivalry between the admirers of the Chengis reached the climax just as the dance neared its peak. Then followed the denouement when the Chengis disappeared for to spend the night in some ivory arms among the silk bed sheets.

The Chengis who were famous for their beauty and seductiveness were like the popular film stars of our day. They were invited to every show and songs were composed for and dedicated to them. Lesbianism was quite widespread in those days. Many wealthy ladies made love to each other and kept tender girls to satisfy their lust in the Harem sections of some rich mansions.

Lesbian Chengis put on a white scarf around their necks to display their inclination. Their love message was embroidered on these scarves with words expressing their longing.

All the leaders of the Chengi troupes wore boots and a white scar and had a fan in their hands which were the inseparable

Beautés orientales. 18/5-19?? Souvenir de Cons/fl

Three girls from a Chengi troupe. late 19th century.

components of their costumes. (Chengis came mostly from the white gypsy communities of the Balkans, though it was not impossible to find some non-Muslim girls who joined these groups.

Istanbul still harbors the traces of this type of entertainment especially in the Sulukule quarter. However it is only a show; there is no trace of lesbianism and both sexes can have their drinks and enjoy it in each other's company.

DANCING BOYS (KÖCHEKS)

The Ottoman male was always after the beauty and charm of youth. He found beauty alluring and captivating both in women and in men. Some Sultans who enjoyed the most attractive and elegant virgin slaves in their Palaces also had fresh and baby-faced lads for their more implicit desires.

The Ottomans favored handsome lads more than the gentle sex and therefore the male dancers were in high demand.

The dancing boys who cheered up the Ottomans' public entertainment places worked in groups similar to the women dancers. These groups were called "Köchek groups" and they, were called by the name of the group leader. Each group usually had 30 dancers and in rare cases this number increased to 200-300 dancers.

Köcheks were the most important entertainers of the Ottoman night life. When their talent was observed, young boys were taught music, dance, and the most important refinements of the profession. These beautiful young guys wore women's clothes and danced for the Sultans on every occasion.

Some of the Köcheks were called 'Bunny Boys'. Their only difference from the other Köcheks was their outfit. They wore a kind of loose pants called 'Şalvar'. Female slaves who were jealous of them danced in the Harem wearing their costumes and pretended that they too were Bunny Boys.

The Köcheks had curly long hair. They dressed up in brightly colored and gold embroidered velvet tops with lace hems and silk skirts with belts. They wore alluring perfumes and some make-up and clicked cymbals on their delicate fingers.

The Bunny Boys wore a black Şalvar and silk tops; and tied a piece of cloth around their waist. The characteristic feature of this outfit was that it reinforced the imagination.

The dance they performed was erotic and provoked the sexual desires of the spectator. The Köcheks danced seductively in accord with the exciting rhythms of oriental music. They usually walked around swiftly prior to the dancing session in order to appeal to the audience. When sensuality got hold of their admir-

Dancing Köcheks. 18th century.

ers; they could not restrain their lust so easily. During this carnal show, the men on the move broke their goblets, yelled at the top of their voices, and they sometimes even molested each other.

Köcheks were always pursued by those admirers who wanted to have sexual intercourse with them.

Some of the Köcheks who had nicknames proper to their bodily grace and temper, appeared on the stage in well-known coffee-houses. When they were unemployed, some of them served drinks to customers in taverns and intoxicated them with their service as well.

The majority of these sexually deviated Köcheks were passive homosexuals. Some of them got married when they got older.

Enderunlu Fazıl Bey portrayed some of the famous male dancers of his age in his book with the title *'Chenginâme'*. Even though the name of his book was "*Chenginâme*" (Dancing Girls), those who were mentioned in it were boys. The reason for this

Dancing Köcheks. Miniature from Surname-i Vehbi. 18th century.

word play was most probably Enderunlu Fazıl's own homosexuality. Here are some excerpts from his descriptive narration:

"The Egyptian's shape and figure is harmonious and unique. He is a Jew. When he starts dancing he drives everybody crazy.

He has got numerous lovers. Even looking at his face or watching him walk around gives you great pleasure but to watch him take off his pants gives you more than pleasure. Yet some of his admirers say that he has got an ugly poop and that his phallus is too big for a Jew."

"Altıntop's (Lit. Golden ball) bottom is always ready for his mates who are always grateful to him."

A dancing Köchek. Late 19th century.

Dancing Köcheks. Surname-i Vehbi. 18th century.

"You get an erection as soon as you see Kanarya (Lit. Canary), he is distinguished."

"Girlish Memed is a wanderer, his property is his ass, and he has thousands of husbands."

BEAUTIES OF THE WORLD THROUGH THE EYES OF THE OTTOMANS

The Ottoman Empire comprised vest countries that stretched out on three continents. Its capital, Istanbul, was one of the most exciting cities of the world where various ethnic groups lived in harmony. The Court always had close relationships with the European countries. Our good old poet, Enderunlu Fazıl Bey, also did civil service as well as writing his five well-known homo-erotic works.

One day, one of his lovers (most probably a very jealous one) inquired "My beloved Fazıl, just to satisfy my curiosity, please tell once and for all which nation's lads are the best and which ones have the largest number of lovers. Write about them and have their beauties illustrated." Fazıl Bey, very much pleased with his loner's wish, wrote his book named "Hubannâme", "The Book of Beauties" on the homosexuals of different nations. How did he visualize the male charmers of various countries? Here are some sections from his book.

Greek Stunners:

Both the men and the women are of a bewitching beauty. 'Their bodies are surprisingly well-built. Oh Lord! What a treat, what a meaningful look. That ivory neck and that raven black hair are unbearable to resist. His chest is like crystal, he is as valuable as pure silver, and he is like strained honey. I can't find enough words to describe the tanned brunettes. There is no trace of hair even on the face of the oldest guy. They walk like courtesans and they can seduce the best men working in the taverns of Galata. You loose consciousness when his locks fall onto his cheeks and if he surrenders, you can die of lasciviousness.

Spanish Charms:

Spain is the inventor of coquetry and the nuisance of the world. Their well-built body is decorated with a pearly complexion and jet-black hair and eye-brows. They have the temper of a Jew. Undouptfully they are charming, howover they are not claver enough to get joy of sex.

A charming English lad. Miniature from Hubannâme. 18th century.

A Russian beauty. Hubannâme. 18th century.

French Beauties:

They are undoubtedly charming; however, they are clumsy in sex. They don't offer any hope for an ultimate union. Do not try to look at them in the eye because their glance is always cast down.

The Flying Dutch:

They are far from being attractive with their frosty skin and

A man of comeliness from Syria. Hubannâme.

they look like the cream-colored Russians. They spend most of their time in the church instead of with their lovers.

British Roses:

They are the silent but very much desired beauties who confuse your mind. They live on a quiet island. These guys who are beardless by birth are of medium height, and are as white as the whitest lily on a stream. Most of these fishlike men are sailors and

Georgian and Austrian graces. Zenannâme. 18th century.

they have a good sexual apparatus; nevertheless, I can not say that they give much satisfaction.

Moroccan Delights:

Tall as saplings, these dark-skinned and violent men are unfriendly. They are unaware of the art of embracing. They are bad tempered and feverish.

Austrian Handsomeness:

Their silver muscles can move the world. They are of European origin. Their limbs are long and fine. They never refuse their lovers. A mole decorates their faces but their hair color is just dull.

Moroccan and Spanish beauties. Zenannâme. 18th century.

Fazıl Bey's lover was delighted with the "Hubannâme" and asked him to write another book but this time on women. The poet refused him by saying, "No prostitute should be mentioned in my fine poetry". When his lover threatened to desert him and decorate the bed of others, Fazıl Bey gave in and wrote the "Zenannâme" (The Book of Women). Here are some examples of his evaluations on a subject he never experienced himself.

Eastern Indians:

Their face, eyes and skin are dark. They look like framed pictures on a wall. You wouldn't feel like having sex with them because they are frigid.

Polish elegance. Zenannâme. 18th century. İ.Ü. Library

Jews:

All of them sleep with us. Jewish women and homosexual boys are abundant. The women have plain faces with a dull skin which is as tasteless as snow.

Greeks Woman:

What a beauty, what a charm! To tell the truth, it is a fortune to have a woman like her. They try all the ways until they turn their lover into a wreck. But they are bad-tempered.

Dutch Women:

Their body is badly proportioned but they walk nicely. They have yellowish complexions and are generally unattractive. Both men and women are alike. All the women are whores.

Poles:

They are outstanding beauties with their passion and you can't take your eyes off her tall gait as she moves. She has a nicely clean and tender body as long as she is not of Jewish descent.

British Women:

When their lips move you hear the nightingale. They are good natured and have lovely faces. They are very keen on finery and they wear sumptuous clothes.

Austrians:

These wicked witches with silky hair and crystal complexions are very capricious.

Spanish Women:

The refined beauties of Spain are tall and slender. Their bodies look very shapely.

French Women:

They are the essence of elegance and have silver skin. They have a pleasant beauty. They always wear fine clothes.

Persians:

Magnificent ladies with almond-shaped eyes; the curves of their body, their eyebrows, their voice and their movements are of an enchanting combination.

Various nations:

Hungarian women are ugly. Never sleep with a Bulgarian. Don't look at Croatians, their lads are good looking but females are cruel.

HOMOSEXUALITY IN OTTOMAN SOCIETY

As we have mentioned, Ottoman men adored beauty and charm without paying attention to the sex of the charmer. Of course this excess addiction gave rise to some problems in the relationship of men and women and was condemned by Islam under all circumstances. Homosexuality was mostly experienced by the educated, upper class, urban inhabitants of the Ottoman society and can be traced in some written texts, poetry and songs.

However, there were also some eminent Ottomans who were disgusted with this practice. A famous historian of the 16th century, Mustafa Ali from Gelibolu (Gallipoli), wrote a book named *'Mevaidü'n Nefais Fi Kavaiddi'l Mecalis'* (Feasts Above the Principles of the Society). In this book, he criticized deviated sexual relationships with uninhibited language.

Here is an excerpt from his book just to give you an idea about his feelings towards those who delighted in homosexuality:

"These wicked people are happy in assholes full of shit and they are convicts. These worthless buggers don't give a damn to anything but screwing a cunt. The perverts are brazen queers. The lesbians who use "zıbık" (artificial male organ) are either the devil's companion or they are the devil themselves. Pimps are dirt and masturbation is only forgery. Procurers and whores are appalling creatures who are after cash. Boys with burning asses and who earn money by their flesh are running in a perilous track. Buggers, wander around to find somebody when their asses get hot and they are good for any kind of obscenity."

The author describes the homosexual men under the headline; "About the boys whose moustache and beard have not appeared yet." In this section of his book, historian Mustafa Ali is somehow more tolerant and includes recommendations such as:" Boys of good quality should not budge an inch from what I have said."

Nowadays, good-looking and good-tempered boys whose moustache and beard have not appeared yet are much more in favor than beautiful and charming women. When a man has a

A beauty from Istanbul. Miniature from Hubannâme. 18th century.

relationship with a woman, he has to keep her behind closed doors and should live this relationship in secret. But still he wouldn't refrain from going out with boys because boys can accompany him wherever he goes; whereas mistresses have to stay in the Harems of the houses.

These young and unfledged boys are mostly bastards from Arabia or orphans from Anatolia. Although the boys of Thrace are generally very tender, the Bosnians and the Herzegovinians are much milder and more easy-going. Hair does not grow on their faces until they are nearly in their 30ies and that makes them very desirable. The freshness of the Arabian and the Anatolian guys is short lived, they can no longer satisfy their lovers when they reach their 20ies.

The best ones come from Edirne, Bursa and Istanbul. These

Effendi and İçoğlanı (Lit. House boy)

A beauty from Istanbul, Levni, 18th century, Topkapı Palace Museum.

guys have very narrow waists and even the ones who are not perfect in beauty have so much charm and cuteness that they are much in demand.

Old and wise men find the unfledged Kurdish boys remarkable. They say that these boys are healthy and easy going, and that they are eager for new tastes. They are even said to decorate their lower bodies with henna, and that they surrender to their lover unconditionally. But the tempting guys of Bursa, Edirne and Istanbul who seem very mild are in fact very calculating. Their wealthy lovers have to pay them a lot of money and doom themselves to misfortune.

It is always possible for two young men to have an affair when they find the right time and place. I do not observe any reluctance when one of the guys makes the other drunk and gives him a good fuck.

To make it short, if you are inclined to lovely-faced tall guys with silvery complexions, stick to the ones from Thrace.

In fact, Herzegovinians and Circassians with their sweet smelling breath are also favored. However the lads of Edirne, Bursa and Istanbul may give you nothing but agony. Albanians are quite stubborn but they know how to ease your heart, whereas Russians and Georgians are far inferior in this respect.

Hungarians make you happy but deceive you as well. I am always perplexed by the Egyptian guys who prefer Abyssinians in bed. They say that both male and female Abyssinians are pure and clean and skillful in love, and that they are fond of showy beds."

The same Mustafa Ali warned the Sultan in a letter by giving a clear picture of the homosexual relationships at the court and asked for precautions:

"Your Imperial Highness,

There is a small mansion at the Topkapı Palace located between the Babü's Saadet (2. entrance) and Bab-ı Hümayun (1. entrance) which serves as a hospital but is used for different purposes. The people in charge of this hospital are obviously practitioners of this dirty intention.

Whenever a boy from the Enderun feels horny, he sends a message to his man and they meet secretly in one of the rooms of the hospital.

The carnage for transporting the sick also gives service to buggers who have been at the hospital before and who even had an affair with the doctor and some staff members there.

The boys of the Palace pay regular visits to this hospital and take turns in order to ease their flesh."

Another group of Ottoman texts is called 'Şehrengiz' and these texts describe the various characteristics of cities like Istanbul, Edirne, Bursa, Belgrade and Manisa, as well as small provinces like Yenice, Yenişehir, Taşköprü, Sinop and Rize. In the texts the poets who dwelled in these cities portray the hand-some and attractive local boys who usually worked in shops and did not conceal their sexual preferences.

There are some 'Şehrengiz's which also describe women but those are very few in number.

Let's have a look at some sections from these texts written in narrative poetry:

The following is from Taşlıcalı Yahya's 'Şehrengiz' on Istanbul.

"A beauty, with lovely eyes.

Admired by the whole world.

This cruel guy is called Kurd Bali.

Spends every moment in his lover's embrace.

He is the perceiver of the earth.

He is like a newborn lamb.

Dancing for a gay customer at a tavern. Hubannâme. 18th century.

90

My life is his life.
If he comes to my bed, I can sacrifice anything.
He burns with desire.
As he batters his lover
He is a brilliant Janissary,
 with a slender figure.
You can not resist his lips
but it is arduous to get a kiss."

Some Ottoman lyric poets declare their homosexuality
in their poems and are openly hostile to the females:
"We are proud poets
There is no room for a whore in our gatherings."
"Thou, powerful man,
don't ever hold onto a dame,
even if she offers thee all the gold of the world.
Tell her to keep the treasure for herself.
She is a harlot, don't be a fool."

"Don't be deceived by the beauty of women
They are false at heart,
evil intriguers,
This is what they, are."

In some of the poems of the lyric poets, we read an unre-
served invitation to their male lovers:
"I beg you for a kiss, don't abstain your face from me Will your
cheeks of red roses be impaired by a kiss?"

"That lover of mine,
When he smiles with lips like rose buds,
How can I wait for the time of love?
I asked for a kiss from my Persian beauty
He said: Why not! But no room is left on my lips".
"His fancy gown of silk and silver,
turns into a drug get cloak
on his satin skin.
I tailored him a rose petal robe
that was too rough for his delicacy.

His silver thighs are stunning.
Is your mother's womb a silver mine?
So fragile is your radiant thigh,
It even gets hurt by the morning breeze.
Men fought fiercely for his legs and tights,
My darling boy's lower half is enough for my satisfaction.
Let his beautiful face belong to others."

Hair growing on a lover boy's face was a very bad sign meaning that he could no longer please his lover with his delicate soft skin. Poets uttered their distress at the sight of hair on the beloved faces in their lines.
"He became mustached,
His beauty is gone but his eyebrows.
The glory of the sun is sunk and gone,
but my eyes still gaze at his half-moon brows."

"Beard appeared on my lover's face but his beauty is not impaired. Even the beard has added to his fame."

Apparently bright and hairless lads were greatly desired but usually lost their charm when their beards grew. One of the main reasons for homosexuality to be widespread in the Ottoman society was the separation of the sexes. Numerous rules and legislations formed huge obstacles between men and women, and naturally young men were left with only one alternative which was their own sex.

WARM NESTS OF LOVE: TURKISH BATHS

Cleanliness was a very prominent issue for the Ottoman society like in any Muslim country. In obedience to the Koran, certain parts of the body are washed and cleaned before the five prayers during the day. It is also compulsive to take a bath after having intercourse. That is the reason why there are so many public baths everywhere, especially in Istanbul.

Ottomans preferred going to the public baths once or twice a week even if they also took a bath at home. Going to the baths was a particularly social event for women. It was a place where they got the latest gossip, showed off with their new costumes, and young unmarried ladies got the approval of their future mother-in-laws.

Baths were also locations of amusement and fun.

When they returned home, they were all rose colored, their hands and feet were decorated with henna, all their extra body hair was waxed off, and they were glitteringly clean and ready to be their husbands' love mate in bed.

Sometimes the physical contact between the irresistible beauties and the masseuses in the bath aroused them, and the bath also* became a secret love nest.

Of course the baths for women and men were separated. The men's bath served other purposes as well. Elegant boys aged between 15 and 17 excited their customers as they took their bath. Other than the boys, tall and stout masseurs worked there to give a massage with a special rough cloth called 'kese' which peels as well. Sometimes they double-relaxed their customers with their huge tool.

The book named "*Dellaknâme-i Dilküşa*" (Heart-Easing Masseurs) is one of the very few Ottoman erotic books which has reached our day.

Author Murat Bardakçı has publicized the full text of this book written by Derviş Ismail Efendi, the Chief Bath Master, 300 years after he deliciously narrated the lives of the boys working in the baths. The characters in the book will greet you now so that you can have a better insight.

Women's bath in Bursa. Jean-Leon Gerome. 1885.

Yemenici Bali (Bali who wears a handkerchief)

'The first boy is Bali who is beautiful, coquettish, good-man-nered, courteous and loyal. He is a rose-bud blossoming for love and a helpless nightingale in your bosom.

His hair is hyacinth, his dimple is like a rose, his looks are an executioner's looks, his tallness is like a boxwood tree, his ass is like a crystal bowl and his navel is a flash of light. This is how he is described.

This unblemished guy, now strolling in the courtyard of the Turkish bath with patterns on his feet was once a shoe-maker's apprentice.

One day as he was walking home in the darkness of the night, the owner of the coffee shop near the caulking place, Gümüş Ali from Darıca waylaid him. He and his companions, sailor Poison Ahmed at the Tophane tyrant, Halil the Wolf, rushed into his honeycomb likes wasps. They fucked his ass until dawn. He was even forced to dance naked.

95

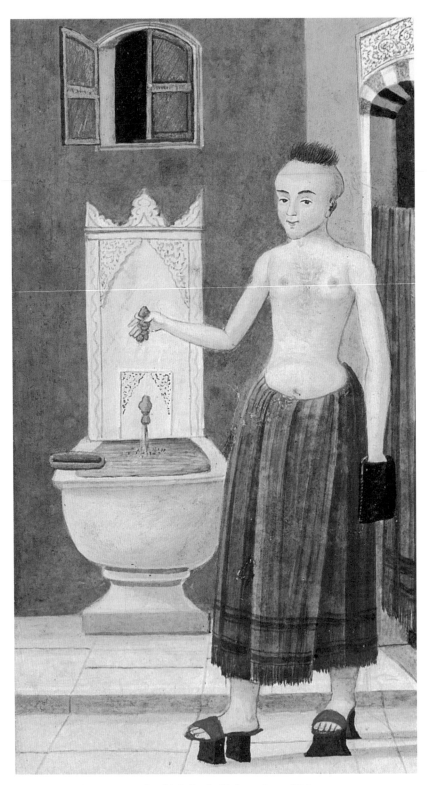

Masseur at a Turkish Bath. Hubannâme, 18th century.

However, their party was spoiled unexpectedly by the Subaşı Ağa (police) who was on duty. He was patrolling when he received notifications about what was going on near the caulking place. He pulled out Yemenici Bali who was lying with his face down under their balls. He even stigmatized his golden name on his buttocks with a mark that read, 'passive boy'.

Yemenici Bali was aware of the fact that the only place where he could go now was the Great Turkish Bath in Tophane which belonged to Kaptan-ı Derya (Admiral) Kılıç Ali Paşa. He received approval from one of the old and wise masseurs by kissing his hand and he took off his clothes.

It took a short time for him to become famous. Now his daytime and evening rates are both 70 silver coins. (70 silver coins are only for one shot). His pimp gets 20 silver coins so it makes 90 silver coins for the customer.

If you want to spend the night with him, you will have to pay 300 silver coins. Then you can screw him up as many times as you can, it is included in the price. But if you wish to go on after the sun rises you will have to pay 90 silver coins extra.

His daytime limit is only three shots. He is a well-built, nice and neat fellow.

Hamleci Ibrahim (Ibrahim the attacker)

Hamleci Ibrahim, who was once a young soldier of the Sultan's Bodyguard division, is always cherished by the homosexuals. This tall guy is like an angel with his hair of golden thread. He has a very slender waist, nicely delicate hands and feet and lips like sugarplums and his nipples are like a drop of amber. His navel is like-hyacinth. If you wish to know about his rear hole, it smells like a carnation.

He lies uncovered in bed or on the white marble floor of the "halvet" (the hottest room in a Turkish bath). He never cares if the penis is too long or too big but takes it in with the power of his youth without any complaint. He refreshes his partner and adds delight to his life. He goes on all night until the sun rises without charge and becomes your fellow-lover in bed. This much loyalty is more than you would expect from a naked bath masseur. He used to live in Giresun, which is a township on the Black

Woman's Public Bath, Ignaze Mouradja d'Ohsson, 1787, Lithograph.

Sea coast. One day his uncle who was an attacker in the Sultan's Bodyguard division came to his hometown and took him to Istanbul. By his favor, he joined the division of the Sultan's Bodyguards. His uncle also found him a part-time job during his training days so that he would not be idle. So he started to work in Barber Salih Çavuş's shop which was at the market place near the Central Customs Quay.

During his apprenticeship in the barber shop, one of the men of the neighborhood saw him with the conic hat of his division's uniform on his falcon head and in his woolen "cepken" (a kind of short overcoat with wide sleeves). His hair on his forehead, his heels like silver ingots, and his pompous walk evoked the feelings of the guy.

This Kurd Haso Ağa, warden of the dungeon, was known as the hairy crazy Kurd and had his eyes on him since quite a time. Sensing this attentiveness, Hamleci Ibrahim also started itching for this man who was thoroughly covered with black hair and was of impressive and high stature.

The Kurd had the agility of a sailor, his strong footsteps shook the earth, and his strong hands could bend steel bars as if they were straws. Most important of all, he had many little boxes full of gold coins.

Being the warden of the dungeon, he came to Salih Çavuş's barber shop on a Friday and asked Hamleci Ibrahim if he would like to pay a visit to the dungeon in the dockyard. The boy followed Haso Ağa to his room eagerly and lost his virginity there. But Haso Aga's penis was like that of a stallion and it was impossible to find a similar one on any of the continents on the earth. When the story was heard by his uncle and Barber Salih Çavuş, he was discharged from the Division of the Sultan's Bodyguards and sacked from Salih Çavuş's barber shop. So he found himself wearing a "peşmetal" (rectangular cloth tied around the waist designating the washers of the baths) at the Yeşildirekli Bath in Azapkapısı.

The customers of this "hamam" were soldiers, dockyard workers and boatmen who were all strong and muscled rascals with

Woman's bath. Zenannâme. 18th century.

100

organs like iron stakes. Whenever they desired Ibrahim, they attacked him like a lion wherever they were; in a private room or in the glass room of the bath. They got what they wanted and gave him what he needed. One shot costs 200 silver coins for distinguished customers. To keep him in bed, one night costs them 1000 silver coins but for only three shots. If he consents to an extra shot, then the fee is 250 silver coins more.

Once we invited him to our house and Yemenici Bali took him to his bed. It was wonderful to witness their passionate foreplay and see them fuck each other alternatingly.

Kalyoncu Suleyman (Suleyman the sailor)

Now let's get acquainted with Kalyoncu Suleyman, who is a big and strong fucker, highly esteemed by the dignitaries. He was born in Trabzon and was reared by his uncles who were sailors too. With a conic hat on his falcon head and a "cepken" which does not even cover his bare chest, he fastened the mooring rope all day and after sunset, and then took off his underwear for his unmarried uncles.

This powerfully built man knows many erotic games in bed, and he is so good at screwing that you feel you can never get enough.

The owner of the Piyale Paşa Bath, Hasan Ağa, saw him once while he was wandering at the Haskoy quay. Hasan Ağa was in Ali Paşa's coffee house with some other sailors who were also gazing at Suleyman and making guesses about the size and the shape of his steel dagger. Suddenly an idea flashed in his mind and he said to himself; this is what I have been in need of, a young, spick-and-span, resourceful and hustling good fucker.' Approaching him with sweet words, he took Suleyman to his bath and wrapped a "peştemal" around his waist with his own hands. Hasan Ağa trained Süleyman for a couple of days and then the lad was ready for the customers.

He is a fucker with manners. He starts the game swiftly and delicately and completes his duty perfectly.

He kindly invites his customer to the 'halvet', hangs a 'peştemal' on the door and puts a pair of patterns in front of it as a familiar sign with an obvious meaning. Then he says; 'Would you please lie down so that I can massage your legs and feet.' When both of them are at the best possible moment, he takes off his 'peştemal' and kisses his customer's feet as he begs: 'My dear master, please have a look at me, you turned me on so very badly, be kind enough to grant this naked slave of yours a little bit of affection.' Turning him face down, he pushes his grand black mallet very slowly and gently until the very end of his patron's ass-hole which really needs ingenuity and this swine has it.

After his good score he kisses his customer's feet again and asks for permission to leave. He is not of the kind who would wait for a tip.

Malleters usually get 100 silver coins for each shot in the baths but even 300 silver coins are too low for Suleyman the sailor.

His nightly visit costs 450 silver coins. He stops if his host says 'enough' after three fucks. But he may offer two more if there is no objection. To get the utmost enjoyment out of these nightly visits, he never hesitates to lie under his host and to entertain him with his asshole.

He is a passionate and valorous man; I mean it.

Peremeci Benli Kara Davud
(Dark and moled Davud the boatman)

Peremeci Benli Kara Davud is another well-known mallet own-er. This strong and tall young man with a newly appearing mous-tache does not have a specific location. He is a mobile fucker who screws notable gentlemen day and night. The profit his mallet makes goes to other screwers and he never keeps anything in hand. He wanders around with bare feet and in old clothes.

When there is a call for him from one of the hamams, he walks to the person in charge of the hamam. After kissing his hand, he goes to the private room where he is expected. If he has met the customer before, he says, 'My dear master, here I am. Your Kara Davud is here!' and then he starts fucking him. But if he has not been acquainted with the customer before, the chief of the masseurs introduces him saying: 'I think he is looking for a fuck-er.' As he is giving him a massage, he also caresses his client's prick tenderly. If the customer says, 'Take your hands off me', he tells him that he is very desirous too, and that there is nothing to

Woman's bath, Münif Fehim.

Turkish Bath. Jéan Leon Gérôme.

be ashamed of, and he shows his big thing. After that, turning the customer face down and finishing up do not take a very long time.

Benli Kara Davud's lover, Kız Cafer (Cafer the girl), is the son of Saraç Ahmet Bey (maker of leather goods) who was once the gate-keeper of Sultan Murad IV's esquire Mustafa Paşa.

Turkish Bath, J. A. Dominique Ingres. 1832.

All the silver coins of Benli Kara Davud are spent on. Kız Cafer whose nickname among the leather workers is masseur's saddler.

Kara Davud does not mind this because he fucks Kız Cafer whenever he wants".

I hope you enjoyed reading how some Ottoman men enjoyed themselves in the baths. Now let us take a look at the women's affaires. Women also had fun in the baths because they were sur-

A Woman on her vay to the public bath (Hamam), Zenannâme. 18th century.

rounded with young and fresh bodies. Besides they made use of the hamams as a meeting place with their lovers. Baron W. Wratislaw who visited Istanbul in 1591 accompanying the Austrian Embassy delegation from Vienna, witnessed how Ottoman women could be very shrewd when they wanted mates, and he noted this event in his diary:

Janissary Mustafa's Adultery

Mustafa had once met a lady and invited her to the Embassy, so I prepared delicious desserts and bought the best wine for this occasion. I liked him because he was originally a Bohemian and he was always nice and polite to me.

Mustafa's lover had an extremely jealous elderly husband who never trusted his wife and who spied on her everywhere she went. But who can stop a woman if she is determined to deceive her husband? Of course, nobody. She used the hamam trick and managed to stick to her appointment.

She told her husband that she was to go to the hamam, and with two of her slaves walking behind her and carrying bundles on their heads, she headed for the bath of Çemberlitas, (this hamam was built by one of the Sultan's legal wives, Ruska Sultan). The hamam is very close to the Embassy, and as she passed by, she signaled to Mustafa which meant that she would attend the invitation on time.

At that time of the day, the bath was at the ladies' disposal and no man could enter unless he wanted to commit suicide. Only her husband who saw green watched her enter the hamam and situated himself in a suitable corner to wait for his wife.

In the meantime, his hot wife changed her green outfit with a red one which was in her bundle. Leaving her slaves in the hamam, she rushed out and went to Mustafa's room. He greeted her happily and entertained her with his generosity very well. After the party she went back to the hamam, washed off her sins, and returned home with her husband and in greens of course.

This little trick of hers always made us burst out laughing whenever we recalled that event.

THE SEX SCANDALS WHICH SHOCKED
THE OTTOMAN SOCIETY:

Sex scandals were not unusual in the Ottoman era although the Islamic rules punished all the parties severely.

Let us now take a look at some of the ones which caused a great social tumult.

The Horny Wife of the Hero:

Bali Bey and his family were renowned for their bravery and warrior ship. They served the Ottoman State especially during the Thracian campaigns.

Bali Bey who was the governor of Semendire, had a wife who come1'from a wealthy, middle-class family. This hero's wife who was a middle-aged beauty was hosting young men in her residence. One day their "konak" was raided and the couple was caught on the spot.

They were taken to the Kadı (judge of the Islamic canon law). The young gentleman confessed the sin before the Kadı and said: "She gives me money, she, feeds me and buys me clothes." So he was registered as the first Ottoman gigolo. But before the Kadı announced his decision on this scandalous adultery, one of the loyal men of Bali Bey took out his dagger immediately and stabbed him and the servants of the house to death.

After this event Bali Bey's honor was more or less restored. His wife was sent to Üsküp (Skopje) to be kept under supervision by a high rank official there.

However, the woman could not stand being away from young boys. She ran away from Üsküp and came back to Istanbul. She started to live together with a young man. They were caught again and the boy was beaten up and sent into exile where he died.

According to the scandalmongers of the age, the hot-headed lady ran to her lover's grave, took his body out of his grave, and made love to his corpse. She then started to live together with her dead lover's brother in Istanbul. This undignified woman was

110

The Couple. Abdullah Buhari.18th century

reported to the Sultan by her neighbors.

But there is no record of Yavuz Sultan Selim's judgement and the rest of the story.

Young Men in Disguise at the Service of the Ladies in the Konaks of Istanbul:

Another scandal shook Istanbul in 1577. A pimp named Mustafa organized the young and attractive boys in the neighborhood of Haliç (Golden Horn) to serve in a special way in the Konaks of Istanbul.

These good-looking and strong boys with long hair entered the Konaks in women's outfit as tailors or hairdressers.

Widows, hornies and young brides who were left alone by their inconsiderate husbands, spent sweet hours in the strong arms of these so-called tailors and hairdressers.

But one day, one of the boys was caught as he was delivering his services. Although he resisted for a long time and remained silent, he confessed everything in the end whereupon Mustafa the pimp was arrested and his team was banished.

A miniature from Hamse-i Atai: A ram scaring the copulating couple.

This distressing revelation caused the gentlemen of the Konaks and all the husbands to become suspicious of their wives for quite a long time.

Besides, 1577 was the year when the divorce rate reached its peak in Istanbul.

Muslim Lady, Jewish Boy, Love and Death

The punishment given to a Muslim woman who committed adultery with a non-Muslim man was to be stoned.

This punishment was given only once throughout the Ottoman era. The wife of Abdullah Effendi who was a retired Janissary, was swooped down with a young Jewish tradesman.

The woman was convicted to death after this event which took place in Aksaray (Istanbul) in 1680.

She was immersed naked in the ground till her waist and was stoned to death by the spectators. This was the first sentence of this kind in the history of the Empire so the notables of the society tried to coax the Kadı of Rumeli, Ahmed Efendi, not to hang the sentence but could not succeed.

The announcement of the crime and the punishment was made public by criers everywhere in Istanbul.

The poor woman was therefore buried halfway in front of the Twisted Column at the Sultanahmet Square and all the people gathered there to stone her to death. Sultan Mehmed IV of the age was said to be among the spectators.

As she was being stoned, the Jewish tradesman was in jail. Even though he converted to Islam and promised to marry her, he could not save his neck from the executioner.

The Lesbian Wife of the Pasha

Osman Paşa who was appointed representative to the Grand Vizier had a well-known lesbian wife. In those days, she was very much in love with a gipsy dancer.

She was the chief figure of the Konak's harem section in Babiali (Istanbul) of course, and she organized crazy parties to entertain herself and her lesbian friends. Her gipsy lover had put a spell on her and was costing her a lot of money. Her poor husband who was very much fond of his wife was buying land for her gipsy lover.

A couple in the Turkish bath. Abdullah Buhari, 18th century.

The inhabitants of the neighborhood and the eminent officials of the state were bothered by this situation.

When Sultan Mahmud II was informed about the reputation of the Paşa's wife, he discharged his office and sent him to Limni and his wife was banished to Bursa.

114

Of course the gipsy girl got her share too. One night she was strangled to death in a deserted street.

A Battle for the Bugger

An ignominious which took place in Istanbul in the middle of the 18th century shook the ranks of the army.

This event brought two divisions of the selected Janissaries of the Ottoman army face to face.

One of the Janissaries had a lover who was a masseur at a Turkish bath. This guy was kidnapped by a Janissary of another division. They spent a couple of days together and had fun. But this caused a bloody fight between the two divisions and the battle took four days.

The Palace could stop this fight only by arresting the masseur and executing him.

Abdülmecid I's Wife of Easy Virtues

Sultan Abdülmecid I ascended the throne in 1839 after his father Mahmud II who had introduced a number of reforms, and proceeded with his father's political reforms. He was one of the most handsome Sultans of the Ottoman Court but unfortunately the only one who is told to have been a cuckold.

In the Harem of the Palace, the least punishment given for refusing the Sultan's will was exile.

Abdülmecid's fourth wife Serefraz was a very jealous woman. She could not stand her husband's indulging in revelry, so she moved to the Yıldız Palace from the Dolmabahçe Palace.

It was said that Abdülmecid who dearly loved Serefraz was not allowed to enter the Yıldız Palace by her order.

Serefraz always dressed up as she wished and went out when she liked. In one of her outings she met an Armenian musician and fell in love with him.

The Armenian guy was invited to the Yildiz Palace and entertained there by Serefraz. The rumor of these visits rattled the city.

But the Sultan was sure that all the talk about his wife was just a lie. One day the Armenian musician was stabbed at the marketplace in Beşiktaş. Even after this scandal, Serefraz remained to be the beloved wife of Abdülmecid I.

THE LANGUAGE OF FLIRTATION

At the turn of the 20th century, the addicts of covert love affairs in Istanbul created a combination of signs and body language against the laws, traditions and punishments that prohibited close intimacy between men and women.

Even though there were some sings of Western culture penetrating through the doors of the Empire, it was still strictly forbidden to have free relationships for both sexes.

Ahmet Rasim who was the outstanding author of the times, shed light upon this unique language as follows:

"When I reached the age of 'making eyes' and playing around I got familiar with the language of love. It wasn't easy, even as a graduate I knew it would take millions of years to complete my PhD thesis. Especially, the pantomime involved was the most difficult part for me. In those days it was not possible to chat or walk side by side in the street, shop together and get on a tram or carriage together with a woman.

I can never forget my friend who was stopped by a policeman because he was seen in a back street talking to a black woman. He had to spend ages at the police station trying to convince the police that the woman was his nanny. Therefore the remote quarters of the city were equally dangerous places to tell your lover, 'you are mine and I am yours.'

This unrecorded language of 'insinuations' was divided into groups such as 'making eyes', 'giving a password' and 'rendezvous'. 'Making eyes' which is a scrap of sign language has also some subdivisions because for both lovers, everything that was worn, and even the style adopted had special meanings depending on time and location, indicating emotions and specific messages.

The sign language played a definite role at leisure, during boat trips at the Bosphorus or in horse carriages, during the stroll in the streets, in following the lover at a near or long distance, in coming across him or her supposedly by chance, during intentional short pauses in the street pretending to fix a shoe

A flirtation is blossoming.

lace, etc., at window peepings, passing by the houses or shops, giving a cough late at night, lighting a match, walking in the street with brisk steps, and at having a piece of paper or a handkerchief in hand. This very evasive communication between lovers evoked all the sexual desires and stimulated the imagination.

Take me for example; when I had a relationship with a lady, and we had agreed on special signs, I would instantly know her intentions from her outfit. It did not matter if her face was veiled; her hair style would tell me where she was headed to. If her hair was arranged in a knot, she was going long distance; if not, she was not. It was that simple. If she was holding her veil, I would meet her very soon in her house but a very conservative costume meant that she was making a formal visit to an important place or was. attending a wedding, perhaps in a far away place like the Bosphorus or the Princes Islands, and that we could not see each other for a couple of days especially if she went away in a carriage.

A change in her usual appearance was a sign of danger; her dressing up like a maid meant that she had got suspicious of me and that she was following me. Combs over the veil or on the hair told me that she had to visit her mother or mother-in-law (because combs mean boredom, even in dreams).

If her hair was sloppy, I had to be careful because it meant that she did not sleep all night because of worrying about me.

Eyes had their own language too. Blinking the right eye once hinted that she was not interested in anything more serious than a flirtation. Signals from the left eye were much more promising, one blink; 'Only one hour left, then I will be in your arms,' whereas two blinks read; 'I will have to wait two hours for the amorous moments.'

If she held her eyelids closed for a spell, I would have to wait for more than an hour, but if the movement of the eyelids were faster, my anticipation was to end in almost half an hour. If she held her fan against her temple thoughtfully, it implied that she was going through a rather hard time but had me in her mind all the same. If she had someone with her at whom she gave a sideways glance, it implied that that person had not gained her confidence; but a smiling gaze towards me meant that she wished to make my existence known to that person.

Do not think I am finished. There are millions of examples of this intriguing language; the number of fingers put on the window of the horse cart, for example, could tell me how many days were left until the end of my longing. A gesture with her hand as if straightening her headdress as she walked meant that she longed to meet me vis-a-vis; an opening and closing gesture of her hands implied that she would pass this way the next day; if she lowered her hand or her umbrella upon seeing me, I were not to follow her; if she pulled on her collar as she passed by and walked briskly, we would be able to meet at a later date; if she held the side of her overcoat or "çarşaf' (cloak) to the front I could follow her discreetly; if she turned back for a momentary look, I could come closer; if she stopped now and then, it meant that her power of endurance was finished.

In short, there was a wealth of meaning for me in every movement, gesture and detail in appearance made at the appropriate moment. But I want you to be sure that mostly these signs were a lot more meaningful than words and more easily understood depending on the nature of your affair.

Do not ever think that a handkerchief is just a worthless piece of cloth. That piece of cloth could be a masterpiece of expressiveness in the hands of a woman in love. Holding it close to her eyes, touching it to her forehead, nose or lips and using it like a fan, could pass on messages: Like: 'I weep1, 'I wish I had not met you', 'You are being unfair', 'My darling, please do not be uncertain of my loyalty', 'Beware of the person next to me', 'Watchdogs are around us, be careful', 'I desperately need you', 'I am keeping my word', 'I want to weep but I can not', 'How many things I wish to tell you, cruel lover', and so forth.

The umbrella held slightly inclined in a boat meant: 'You have hurt my feelings.' More so: 'I swear I am broken-hearted, I will not talk to you.' If it covers the entire face: 'You will not see me again', 'I do not want to see you again, haven't you understood yet?'

The umbrella is moved from right to left: 'Go on, do not stop!' Falls forward a little: 'I am getting excited again.' Moves backwards: 'Look!' Falls back: 'See how I feel! Have pity.' Moves sideways: 'Oh! What happiness!' Is opened and shut: 'We will fix the

Ladies of Istanbul on the vay to an outdoor entertaintment. Mahmut Kılıç.

Signalling the lower with a dropped handkerchief. Yüksel, author collection.

day later.'

Evasive greetings, frowning, every kind of meaningful gazing, sighing, wetting the lips, trembling, biting the lips and pouting, sucking, swallowing, all the ways of shaking the head, putting her hand on her heart, deep sighs, deep breathing with closed eyes, little smiles, deep laughter gazing down, shutting the eye after a deep look and pretending not to see were all sentences of this secret language. Putting the index finger on the lips to indicate; 'I have something to tell you'. Sitting with a frowning of the pouty face, body down with a bent neck; 'we will be observed, please do not look.' Putting the elbows at the side of the boat and sitting with the fist to the temple with a neck bent, whispering things to the person sitting next to her, suddenly gazing at the other boats passing by, and slowly lowering the eyelids like paying thanks; 'Cruel, do not make me talk. My heart is full.' Talking with loving gestures to her neighbor while gazing at you in a hidden manner.

In short all of these are the 'mimicry' belonging to a very special kind of language. Every feeling, acquaintance, first rendez-vous, hurt feelings, breaks and all pleasurable feelings would be expressed through gestures. Poems and letters would be written on these basic indications, news, thanks, aroused interests, pleadings, excuses, competitions and jealousies would be expressed within the framework of this sign language.

The finesse involved in expressing thoughts and feelings in this manner has disappeared. There is no longer any need for the quick expression of the desire of the spirit. Adultery is openly performed in the streets, in lonely ruins, at the beaches, and in the shadow of the trees."

The earlier style of adultery could not bear to be recognized by a single stranger's eyes; if it could have eyes to see our modern times, it would be red hot with shame.

A saddening intercourse. A. Buhari, 18th century manuscript.

OTTOMAN SEX ANECDOTES

The tradition of telling anecdotes has always had an important role in Turkish literature. After the 16th century, some of the anecdotes were collected and written down and now they are as valuable as crystal balls which reflect social life maybe much better than the work of historiographers.

Turkish anecdotes can be divided into two main groups: Anecdotes about well-known characters like Nasreddin Hodja, Incili Çavus, and Bekri Mustafa and anecdotes about ordinary people. Anecdotes about sex could be included in this second group. But in this section of the book the hero of the sex anecdotes is Nasreddin Hodja who was the philosopher of the simple people. However, it is very doubtful that he is the real. hero of these anecdotes. There are also some obscene anecdotes about the poet Namık Kemal, the leader of the Young Turks movement and a philosopher brave enough to challenge the Sultans. Perhaps being the hero of such anecdotes was what he got from the public in return for his bravery.

Answer me!
- One day Nasreddin Hodja was caught with a woman in bed and taken to the Kadi (Judge). The Kadı was surprised to see the Hodja and asked: "Is that really you Hodja who committed this terrible deed?" Instead of answering the Kadı, the Hodja took out his prick and said: "You were so enthusiastic, I could not follow your ins and outs, now you answer the Kadı's question."

Sesame Oil
- Two women approached Nasreddin Hodja one day and they said: "Dear Hodja, in the dark we urinated in two separate jars. Now there is urine in one of them and sesame oil in the other. We can't tell which one belongs to whom." The Hodja coolly answered them: "It is very easy to tell, come near me and take off your clothes. I'll squeeze your pussies, and find out the source of the sesame oil."

125

The Minaret

- The Hodja saw a long minaret in a big city and asked the inhabitants what it was called. The men around replied with the purpose of teasing him: "This is the penis of the city!" Then the witty Hodja asked: "Do you have a proper asshole for this?".

The Donkey

- Ahmed saw a female donkey resting in a cave. He walked behind the donkey and started fucking her but he was swooped down by the owner of the animal. He asked: "What on earth are you doing Ahmed?" Ahmed replied: "To do you a favor, I am trying to raise her up with my prick, and you should pay for my service."

Save Your Donkey from the Wolves

- While Mehmed was having sex with a donkey, its owner appeared, and was stunned by Mehmed's act. Mehmed wanted to calm him down and said: "Don't worry, a good fuck won't hurt your friend but beware of the wolves".

Mourning

- The Hodja's wife came home one day and saw that all her belongings were stolen. She took off her pants and began to talk to her cunt: "My prosperous cunt, you are my treasure. I owned whatever I had in life with your help. There is no reason for sorrow; I'll gain more than I had as long as you are my pal."

When the Hodja came home and heard everything his wife had said, he went out and pulled his pants down. He also started a dialogue with his cock: "You devil, you nuisance, you troublemaker, you are my misfortune. In the future you will be my grief.

Hearing the Hodja's cry, his wife came out and asked: "My dear husband, what is the problem?"

The Hodja got mad and said: "Woman! Have I joined in your cunt's wedding? Why do you indulge in my cock's mourning?"

The Destiny of the Beggar

- One morning the Hodja woke up and wanted to make love with his wife. He told his wife to hold her legs up and got ready

to dive in but at that moment he heard the call for the morning prayer. So he told her not to change her position until he came back and left. While his wife was waiting for the Hodja with her legs up and wide apart, a beggar knocked on the door. There was no answer but the realized that the door was not locked and he walked in saying, "Help this poor creature of God." Then he saw the woman in bed ready for a fuck and he thought that this was the alms of God. As he was working hard on the Hodja's wife, he came back from the morning prayer and found them in bed. The Hodja said: "This is the faith of the beggar my God, everbody has his own l(f)uck."

The Field

- The Hodja had a cultivated land but crows were always there to spoil his crops, so he decided to stay there at night to save his land from the crows. In the darkness of the night he heard his daughter's voice flirting with her boyfriend. Her lover said: "Let's play a game. I'll be the stallion and you will be the mare." They started the game being unaware of the Hodja's presence there. As they were at the hottest spot, the stallion noticed the Hodja's wide open eyes staring at them and he began to run away. The disappointed mare ran after her stallion with a piece of greenery in her hand and yelled: "Come back, come back!"

When the Hodja saw his desperate daughter, he declared: "My stupid girl, do you think that the guy who was as faithless to a cunt as white as cream will return for a bit of grass!"

Let Me Free

- The Hodja's wife asked her husband who came back from the evening prayer: "What was the preaching about?" The Hodja told everything to his wife: "He who makes love to his wife at night gains divine recompensetion as if he has sacrificed a sheep for God. He who makes love to his wife at midnight does not have to sacrifice a camel for the good will of God, and if he makes love to his wife early in the morning, he is as dear as a wealthy man who freed a slave for the sake of God." Then the time came for bed. She said: "My beloved Hodja, let's acquire merit in God's sight "and so they did. She woke up in the middle of the night and

asked he for another meritorious action and he said OK. Early in the morning she, woke up as hot as fire and told him: "Let's free a slave, my dear husband".

The dispersed Hodja who could do no more for the will of God begged her: "I am your slave now, please set me free."

Being in Love

A Bektashi was asked one day; "Have you ever been in love?" He said: "Yes, I almost was once but her husband walked in and we could not embrace each other."

The Sin

Walking with bare feet on his long journey, a Bektashi saw an old and unsightly woman on top of a hill. Because he was deprived of sex for months, the woman seemed as beautiful as an angel to him and he made love to her. He looked at her face once more after he finished and realized how ugly she was. He said; "Oh Lord! Is this act of mine going to be recorded as a sin?"

The Collar of the Shirt

Poet Zati was going to the thermal baths in Bursa with his male lover who was a bright young lad. He met a couple of female acquaintances of his. Zati's bugger wanted to tease the ladies and asked: "Have you got any shirts with open collars?" One of them answered: "Our open collars are now out of fashion but your turtleneck is much more esteemed these days."

The Zıbık (Dildo)

Once upon a time there was a craftsman in the Covered Bazaar who earned his living by making wooden "zıbıks" which were very much demanded by the women of Istanbul. One day a slave girl went to his small manufactory. He asked: "How can I help you, my dear girl?" She said: "My Lady has a request from you!" "What type?" he asked and she answered: "I don't know how to define it, but My Lady said she wants a zibik as big as the Turk's,

An unhappy wife is complaining to the Kadi about her husband's impotence her evidence is a zibik (hand made artificial male organ). Miniature from Hamse-i Atai.

129

at the same time, as black as an Arab's and tall and tapering like an Albanian's, as dexterous as a Laz's. She wants it to be hairy like a Kurd's and it should be as agile as a Circassian's, and as gentle as a European's and it must be vigorous like a Venetian's and..." The zıbık-maker stopped her and said; "My dear girl, tell your lady, if I find one like that I'll screw my own ass with it."

We Did What You Did But We Could Not Perk Him Up

A physician was crossing through a village on the Black Sea coast. Suddenly he heard screams and cries calling for a physician. He approached the person desperately looking for help and asked: "I am a physician, what is the matter?" The man named Temel answered him in haste: "My wife Fadime died. We married yesterday and we were in our bridal chamber, but the moment she lost her virginity, she bellowed and died."

The physician asked for permission to go into the room she was in an4 closed the door, Fadime was lying in bed, and her beautiful body was all bare. He realized that she had only fainted and helped her to recover. Then the newly married bride and the trespasser fell on the bed, made love for a long time, and he left the room. All the villagers and Temel were waiting for him anxiously in front of the door. The exhausted physician came out and said: "I worked very hard but I managed to bring her back to life."

A year later, he was passing by the same village accidentally and Temel saw him and said: "Hey doc! Your treatment did not work on the barber. He died last month, and all the men of the village have been fucking him since then but we could not perk him up yet."

WHAT TYPE OF LITERATURE DID THE OTTOMANS ENJOY READING?

In the previous sections of our book we have mentioned the Bahnâmes which were books on sex. Now let us have a look in the other written texts which were the Ottomans' beloved classics on the bedroom shelf.

Mevlana Jelaleddin-i Rumi, the founder of the order of the 'Whirling dervishes', wrote a book named 'Mesnevi' which is an example of such books. In his Mesnevi, he mentioned sex in didactic versifications when he portrayed and commented on human characteristics and his stories were always concluded with morals.

Here are some excerpts from Mevlana's "Mesnevi": '

The Donkey Story

Once upon a time, there was a prurient slave girl who always starved for sex and her desire was never satisfied. She found the cure in a donkey, and trained him to copulate with her. This willing girl used a calabash to shorten the length of the donkey's tool. She did this to get only half of its grand prick in her as the don-key fucked her because his huge organ would tear her womb apart and kill her.

One day the lady of the house realized that the donkey was losing weight and getting weaker and weaker. She decided to find the reason why. Anybody who is decisive enough to know the truth, will of course reach his goal in the end, and this was exactly what she did. One day she saw the slave girl under the donkey and she was green with jealousy. The donkey was fucking the slave girl like a passionate man.

The lady of the house said to herself: "I am the owner of this ass, I should be the one who is having the fun, not the slave girl." One day she decided to realize her will of being the donkey's lover and sent the slave girl away from home. She was thrilled with lust: "Thank God for this moment of being alone with my partner, I am released from my husband's superficial and inadequate fucks." She was full of lechery, and this made her blind and deaf, and the donkey became the most attractive mate.

Inordinate desire turns the beast into a beauty, and lust is the worst of the disasters which turns a good reputation into wretchedness and smartness into sturdiness.

The lady of the house locked the door with care, held the animal close to herself and led him to the center of the stable. She closed her eyes for the moment of joy, lying down on the pedestal just like her slave. The ass held his back foot up and dived into the lady of the house with the full length of his penis. Her lungs tore apart and her veins busted with the haste of his drive, and death came just before her last breath. Have you ever seen somebody killed by a donkey's prick?

When the slave girl came back home she witnessed the tragic doom of her mistress and she started screaming: "Oh! My Lady, you have seen the cock of the ass, why haven't you seen the calabash?"

Before you start doing something, complete your observations. Otherwise, you will end up in a catastrophe.

Veiled Cuha In Wraps

There was a preacher once whose words were powerful and who had the gift of the gab. One day he was preaching on the pulpit in a mosque. Women and men who gathered around him were listening to him. Cuha wrapped himself up and covered his face with a veil and sat among the crowd. He was not recognized by anyone. There was a lady sitting next to him and she besought: "Dear preacher, please enlighten me about the length of pubic hair. How long should it be so that my daily prayer can be accepted by God."

The wise reverend answered; "If you're pubic hair is longer than barley, your prayer is profane. Shave it or wax it off when it gets longer than barley." Hearing the answer of the preacher, Cuha drew near her and said, "I request your help, sister. Could you please test the length of my pubic hair?" Her hand dipped into his loose pants and as soon as she grasped his prick she bellowed. The preacher asked when he heard her yell: "Did my words move your heart?"

A delicious night. Münif Fehim.

"No," said Cuha, "It is not her heart but just her hand."

Jelousy

Once upon a time there was a man who had a jealous wife and a slave girl who was beautiful like an angel. His wife was always cautious not to leave the two alone.

But fate is unavoidable; she went to the public bath with the slave girl but then she realized that she had forgotten her silver bowl at home. She told the slave girl to go and fetch it.

The girl had been longing for this moment for six months and she quickly rushed home to meet her master who was alone at home.

They could not even close the door, embraced each other instantly and started to make love. At that moment the wife realized the big mistake she had made, rushed out of the hamam, and put on her outfit to go.

Do you think emotions of love and fear could be placed side by side? What is the difference between them? Love is the reflection of God whereas fear is the counterpart of lust.

When she ran into the house, the lovers heard the sound and parted. She found the slave girl like a wreck and her husband praying. She got suspicious and held up her husband's skirts and saw semen on his balls and penis still dripping on his knees. She yelled; "What an inferior man you are, are those the balls of a man in prayer?"

The morale of this story is; even your own testicles can be the proof of your lie.

134

FETTAHNAME

I was a charming lass of sixteen,
I lived in a mansion in Bağlarbaşı.
Days were passing by as I longed for adulthood
under the pine trees against the breeze of Çamlıca.
We had a cook named Ali Fettah.
He made helva[1] every year with the right savor.
He was always by my side and chased me everywhere.
We strolled in the plains and paced the flowerbeds.
Together we had fun and burst into laughter.
We played the game of hide and seek,
and I rested my tiredness on his chest.
Tenderly he caressed and cast kisses on my braids,
ponderous fingers of his felt every portion of myself.
As years went by I became a devotee of this harmony.
Unless I was in his view, he was idle like a drone.
I grew up, leaving the years behind,
intuition of vitality ornamented my robustness.
My eyelashes were dancers,
and my glance was a blaze,
the blossoming tits of mine were restless.
My rejoicing laughter was shingles of gaiety.
I knew I was no more a bairn
and a strange feeling made me search for a male.
My dreams were mystified

---

(1) A Turkish dessert made of sugar, butter and flour.

but my daydreams were filled with neighborhood lads.

I was once in the garden with my desirous heart

and lay on Fettah's bundle,

I felt a puffy under his slacks

for the first time, and astounded I touched.

Fettah was in a lull, I adjoined

slowly moved the puff, I was instantly listless.

"What is that Fettah, quivering around?" I asked

timidly he said, "My Lady, that is my prick"

"No", I said "That is out of my trust,

As far as I know a penis is as tiny as a thumb."

"Fettah ", "I said ", I must see it.

You know my meddling, if I do not observe, I will be down.

Caressing my hands he took off his pants,

the first thing I saw was a pear-shaped head

then a pink trunk came out.

Fettah was expounding as I stayed in trance.

"It is a kind of handy cane made of flesh,

semen is moved up by the balls down below,

endears the fanny and slides into the pussy.

The biggest one is called 'mallet'

women still hanker after,

it is a golden calf for which females die.

More than joy you get when you have it.

I was fumbling his prick while I was listening,

as I was enfolding with his penis it got harder like a rock,

with the majesty of its steepness it was slowly shaking.

Fettah was in moans, swaying.

At last he held me tight,

squeezed my fanny, kissed my wrists.

Seated me on his lap and leaned sideways,

pressed his mallet in the middle of my ass.

He shuffled along on my pants

but I got no pleasure out of this nanny game.

Shortly afterwards he laid hands upon my pants,

he pulled it down and tore it up,

grasped my unjaded fanny and said:

"Come closer My Lady, let me show you the dexterity

of my mallet".

And nudged his prick into my asshole.

His was not a mallet but an arrow of flesh and bone.

Fettah was sucking my nipples as he was murmuring,

"I am coming, I am coming!"

For an unknown reason I was in a brandished state.

My expectant soul vas anticipating more than that

neither honey nor helva was sweeter than this petting.

Then the massive mallet hollered.

Milky juice erupted from its pear-shaped head

and messed up my ass.

Soon it bowed and scraped with modesty.

I was disillusioned after all the endeavor

and I asked "What pleasure I got out of that ?"

Fettah was the scholar so I should be his apprentice.

Therefore I kissed his lips and said:

"My almighty hero, my old and loyal man,

you are my source, my support, my ground,

سهٔ بر بر میم سرخ ایل نازند انی
برم انتم جلاه آنه طرفیں کریم آس
ننام کرتی فرایسه برحالم باخوردهٔ
ناشیم وایالانتم، حایس آخوردهٔ

لوکنده طیابرکی آمعسم یرنجی آب
لانتم ددوبردره کهٔ فرنم برآدبلجّم
فراه ددود نجاب آنغُ آتر بناطشی
اوکنه برجنام آتر انتا قهٔ ارلا شده

اورار آسمه را ادبنه ماسوس وفرنظار رام
سمر مرم بانی سربکزیردبم طوازلازه
دراسل برایت نه زرهبی ناشه نه ادربه
دات را اسهبی بر مزرم آخور رم

An original page from the manuscript of the Fettahnâme.
Collection of the author.

I beseech you, please make me come.

My words overwhelmed him.

His powerful arms holding me tight,

he removed my skirt and kissed my thighs

he bit my lips and squeezed my tits,

then his face was between my thighs

he licked my cunt,

he found my button and pressed it with his tongue.

I was unconscious, thunderbolts danced in my brain.

Then I reached the peak,

an unbearable gluttony.

I lay on the grass, I was worn out.

As the moments went by

I was aroused, the sparkle in me

turned into a bonfire, I said:

"I am ravenous for what you have done,

I want to have it once more

but this time by your hammer."

"Be lenient, My Lady," he said,

"You will be a bride soon.

Your husband is the one to fulfill your desire

I wish your dreams will come true and

you will always ask for more.

When the prick enters,

its head hurts your vulva a little bit

but the rest will glide in, then

all barriers are gone.

In this world, it is the sweetest job ever known.

Young lads have modest ones,

but ladies never favor modesty.

The medium one is called a cock,

the biggest one is a mallet

which stirs the cunt.

Addict vapids die for it!

I am always after knowledge

I must find out if Fettah's is a hammer or not.

As far as he told me a prick is a lot pettier,

but I think his hammer is much bigger.

If it is so, no more years waiting for bride hood,

I must have it in my cunt or else he will not be free.

With these thoughts in my mind,

I got hold of his organ

and my lips were kissing his,

at the same time we were one,

rocking like sailors in a boat.

His huge hand got hold of my thigh

and twirled sideways my buttock.

He, resting my leg on his shoulder gently,

and with his vigorous strength,

rammed his hard tool into mine.

We rose and fell on the grass

until we came together with a cry.

Let my virginity be yours, I claim nothing

but this pleasure of the soul.

I am willing everyday

for to curry favor with your tool.

BIBLIOGRAFY

Ahmet Rasim   : Fuhş-i Atik. İskit Yayınları, İstanbul 1958.
Ali Rıza Bey   : Teşrifat ve Teşkilatımız. Tercüman 1001
                           Temel Eser, İstanbul.
Meral Altındal   : Osmanlı'da Harem. Altın Kitaplar Yayınevi,
                           İstanbul 1993.
Meral Altındal   : Osmanlı'da Kadın. Altın Kitaplar Yayınevi,
                           İstanbul 1994.
Altıntaş, Günel (Haz.)   : Müstehcen. Soyut Yayınları, İstanbul 1975.
Bardakçı, Murat   : Osmanlı'da Seks. Gür Yayınları, İstanbul 1994.
Burhanettin Semi   : Aşk - Çeşitli Açılardan. İstanbul 1973.
Croutier, Alev Lytle   : Harem - The World Behind the Veil.
                           Abbeville Press, 1989.
Ertop, Konur   : Türk Edebiyatında Seks. Seçme Kitaplar,
                           İstanbul 1977.
                         : Çağlarboyu Anadolu'da Kadın. T.C. Kültür
                           Bakanlığı, İstanbul 1993.
Eyüboğlu, İsmet Zeki   : Divan Şiirinde Sapık Sevgi. Okat Yayınları 1968.
Gelibolulu Mustafa Ali   : Görgü ve Toplum Kuralları Üzerinde Ziyafet
                           Sofraları. Tercüman, İstanbul 1978.
Hiçyılmaz, Ergun   : Eski istanbul'da Muhabbet. Cep Kitapları. İstan-
                           bul 1989.
Hiçyılmaz, Ergun   : Çengiler, Köçekler, Dönmeler, Lez'olar. Cep
                           Kitapları, İstanbul 1991.
Koçu, Reşad Ekrem   : Osmanlı Tarihinde Yasaklar. Tarih Dünyası
                           Mecmuası Yayınları. İstanbul 1950.
Koçu, Reşad Ekrem   : Yeniçeriler. Koçu Yayınları, İstanbul 1964.
Koçu, Reşad Ekrem   : İstanbul Ansiklopedisi. I-XI. cilt, İstanbul 1958-
                           1971.
Mevlânâ Celaleddin   : Mesnevi. Milli Eğitim Basımevi, İstanbul 1945.
Olivier   : Türkiye Seyahatnamesi. Ayyıldız Matbaası,
                           Ankara 1977.
Sevengil, Refik Ahmet   : İstanbul Nasıl Eğleniyordu. İletişim Yaymları,
                           İstanbul 1990.
Scognamillo, G.   : Beyoğlunda Fuhuş. Altın Kitaplar Yayınevi,
                           İstanbul 1994.

Uluçay, Çağatay	: Osmanlı Sultanlarına Aşk Mektupları. Tarih Dünyası Mecmuası Yayınları, İstanbul 1950.
Uluçay, Çağatay	: Harem'den Mektuplar. İstanbul 1956.
Uluçay, Çağatay	: Osmanlı Saraylarında Harem Hayatının İçyüzü. İnkılap Kitabevi. İstanbul 1959.
Uluçay, Çağatay	: Harem II. Türk Tarih Kurumu Yayınları. Ankara 1985
Ünver, A. Süheyl	: Levni. Milli Eğitim Basımevi. İstanbul 1951.
Wratislav, Baron W.	: Anılar. Karacan Yayınları. İstanbul 1986.

Book of Shehzade

BOOK OF SHEHZADE
By MEHMED GAZAL
144 p. 14.5x21.5 cm.

This book is an Ottoman legend, one that has managed to preserve its mystery for 500 years.

The book you hold in your hands is a book that is considered the most mysterious and has garnered the most reaction in dealing with the subject of sex in the east.

Its name is listed third after the masterpieces The Perfumed Garden and Kama Sutra that you have heard about or read, whereas it is more frank and realistic. The realites of Mehmed Gazali, who screamed all about a world of uninhibited sex, have only been imagined in the 20th century. The book delves into the love between Adam and Eve, the roots of homosexuality, the warfront between the pederasts and womanizers, bestiality, voyeurism from pimps to horny women, horny transsexuals with men.. in short, everting you wanten to know about sex but were afraid to ask.. sorry, the explicit sexual adventures of those who experienced a myriad ways to get off.

Oriental Belly Dance

The oriental belly dance is an unequalled exhibition which tells the story of man's birth. The oriental belly dance is the rhythmic expression of the female capacity to give birth and her desire for sexual intercourse. In other words, it is the feminine expression of the human being's basic instinct to perpetuate his race.

This universal feeling is the reason why belly dancing is globally accepted, appreciated and applauded.

The "belly jerk" routine, from which the dance derives its name, is a rendition of a fetus kicking its mother's belly and symbolizes pregnancy. This dance, which was born on Anatolian soil some 8,000 years ago, is nothing but a demonstration of the happiness felt at the emergence of a new life. Belly dancing is generally accepted to be the sensuous exposition of the female's instinct to seduce the male and is, in this sense, a sacred call.

The oriental belly dance is the most powerful aphrodisiac humanity has ever discovered and cherished...

ORIENTAL BELLY DANCE
By KEMAL ÖZDEMİR
160 p. 16x24 cm.
Full Colors